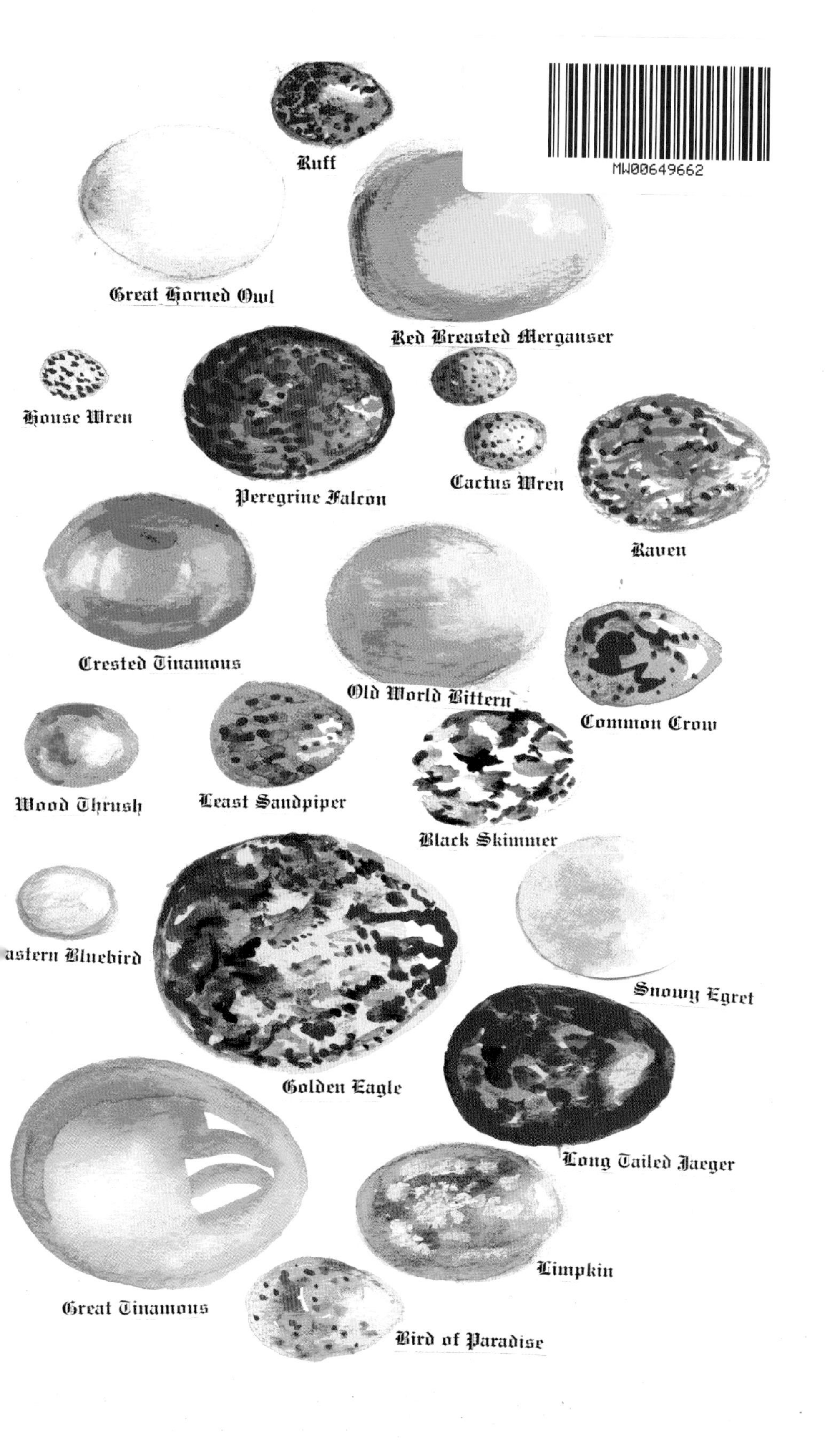
MW00649662
Ruff
Great Horned Owl
Red Breasted Merganser
House Wren
Peregrine Falcon
Cactus Wren
Raven
Crested Tinamous
Old World Bittern
Common Crow
Wood Thrush
Least Sandpiper
Black Skimmer
astern Bluebird
Snowy Egret
Golden Eagle
Long Tailed Jaeger
Limpkin
Great Tinamous
Bird of Paradise

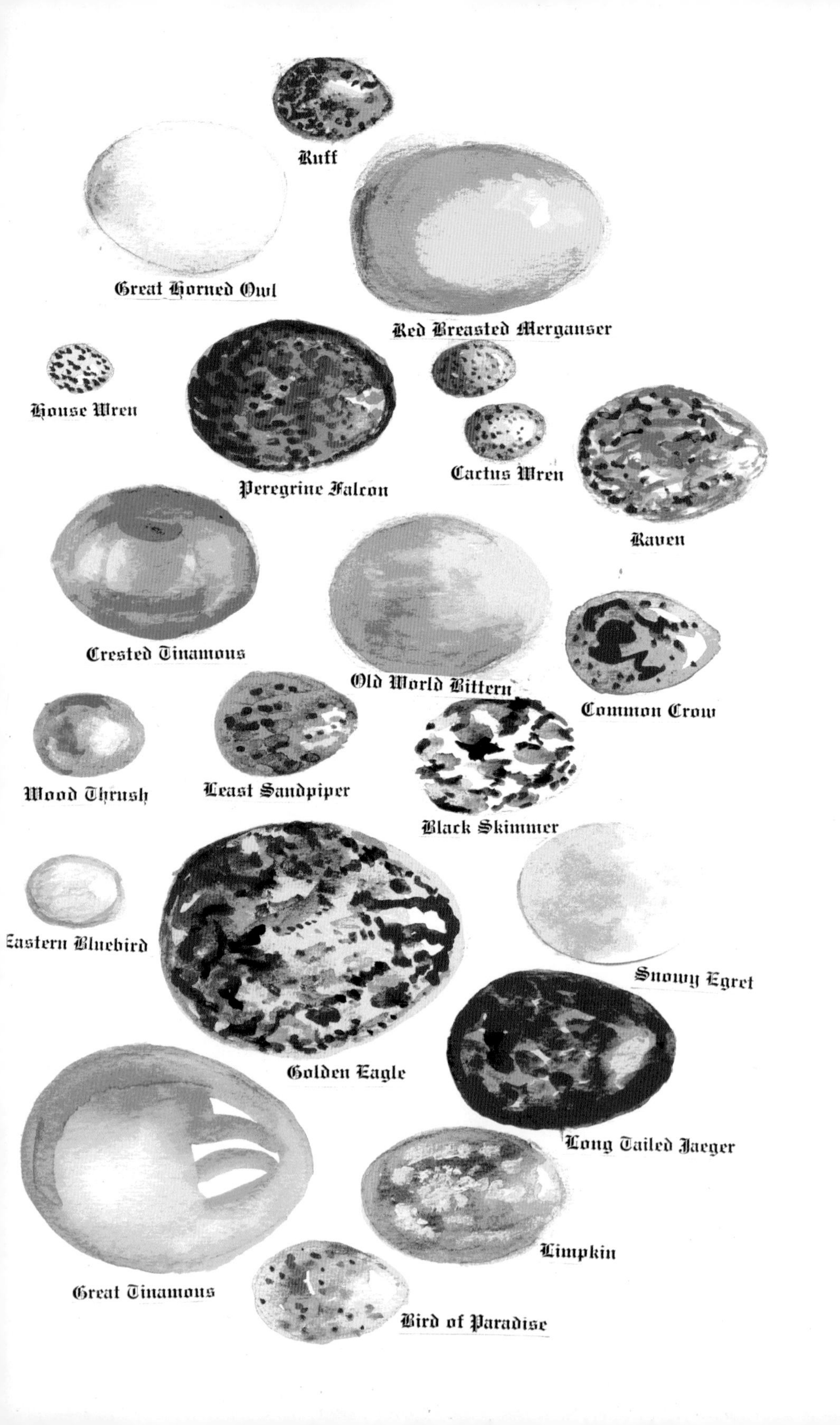
Ruff
Great Horned Owl
Red Breasted Merganser
House Wren
Peregrine Falcon
Cactus Wren
Raven
Crested Tinamous
Old World Bittern
Common Crow
Wood Thrush
Least Sandpiper
Black Skimmer
Eastern Bluebird
Snowy Egret
Golden Eagle
Long Tailed Jaeger
Limpkin
Great Tinamous
Bird of Paradise

BIRDS OF THE CARIBBEAN

(second edition)

One hundred and eleven watercolor paintings with text, describing the habitat, food, history and origins of the birds who reside in the Caribbean or rest there temporarily

By Lucy Baker

(Who lived in the Caribbean for 25 years).

BOOKS by Lucy Baker

1. In Six months you get Bananas,
   I.S.B.N. 978-976-8056-85-6 $14.95
2. Miracles,
   I.S.B.N. 978-1-929440-00-9 $14.95
3. Heart of Stone,
   I.S.B.N. 978-1-929440-5-4 $14.95
4. Dark Before The Dawn,
   I.S.B.N. 978-1-929440-10-8 $14.95
5. Poppelsdorfer Allee,
   I.S.B.N. 978-929440-11-5 $24.95
6. Secrets of Lost River,
   I.S.B.N. 978-1-92440-01-6 $14.95
7. Journey Towards The Light,
   I.S.B.N. 978-1-92440-06-1 $19.95
8. Birds of The Caribbean,
   I.S.B.N. 978-1-929440-17-0 $19.95
9. Treating Ailments With Plants & Her $14.95
   I.SB.N. 978-976-9501-62-1
10. Poisonous Caribbean Plants,
    I.S.B.N. 978-1-929440-03-0 $14.95
11. Fish of the Caribbean
    I.S.B.N. 978-1-929440-04-7 $14.95
12. William Grayson and the Consititution,
    1788, I.S.B.N, 978-1-929440-13-9 $24.95
13. Letters and Speeches of William Grayson

SCREENPLAYS

Miracles
Heart of Stone
The Life of William Grayson

How they delight you + me: the birds, Lucy Baker

BIRDS OF THE CARIBBEAN

Permanent Residents,
Winter visitors from the
North & those that rest
in the islands before flying
to other islands, further south

Nautilus Publishing Company
Since 1981

Library of Congress Cataloging in
Publication Data

Title: Birds of the Caribbean, 2nd edition
Author: Lucy Baker
I.S.B.N. 978-1-929440-17-7
L.O.C. PCN number:
2008929700

Artwork throughout and cover design
by the Lucy Baker
with graphic editing by
Alan Hammerschmidt

Nautilus Publishing Company, siince 1981

This book is dedicated to all who love the creatures of the air, who believe that flying is a thrilling feat, reserved for God's most well loved creatures. I chose these species for their bright, elegant plumage and unique characteristics. This project gave me great pleasure because I do so love the birds.

I lived on St. Maarten in the Caribbean for 25 years And often went bird watching. Many of the birds featured in this book inhabit St. Maarten and the neighboring islands, Saba, Anguilla, St. Barth's, St. Eustatius, St. Kitts and Nevis.

Some birds only stop over in St. Maarten before flying on to South America. Occasionally a few of them nest and lay their eggs on the island, which makes them inhabitants.

The Caribbean Islands have a great number and variety of sea birds who are a complete delight to watch.

A couple of hundred years ago the mongoose was imported to many of the islands to kill the snakes that were brought to keep slaves from running away. The mongoose found it easier to eat the song birds and wiped out almost all of the species except the sea birds who escaped. Slowly the land birds have re turned.

Many tame parrots escaped from cages and live wild in the mountains of the various islands, eating berries, seeds, flower petals, and sharpen their beaks on bark. Sometimes they can be re-captured, especially those who Have forgotten or never learned how to live free.

Art work throughout the book
was executed by the author,
Lucy Baker
including the birds and the cover.

Where possible the birds were researched in their habitats in the Caribbean. The author lived on St.Maarten for 25 years

TABLE OF CONTENTS

DEFINITIONS

DIMORPHIC: Having two body types, male and female being the same.

EPIPHYTES: An organism that grows on or attaches to a living plant; bacteria, fungi, algae, lichens, mosses, ferns.

AQUATIC EPIPHYTES: Seaweed is one and angiosperms.

DUIRNAL: Feeding, flying, hunting during the day.

NOCTURNAL: Feeding, flying, hunting during the night.

ERECTILE CREST: Bushy head feathers, pointed or stiff.

COVERTS: Feathers that cover the base of a main wing feather. The upper side of the wing remex is covered by a greater covert which is likewise covered by a median covert and then by the minor coverts.

VENT: The undermost lower part leading to the private parts; often a different color than the belly or back.

CERE: fleshy ,otfen waxy like structure at the base of the beak between the lores.

LORE: The space between the eye and the bill, bare of feathers in many species.

FLEDGLING: a young bird that is ready to leave the nest and become inependent.

CHICK: Newly hatched baby bird.

MIGRATORY: Birds that fly to another clime,usually going from cold to warm weather. Where they breed is their home.

BARRING: stripes, bars of color,often black or brown that define or edge.

JESSES: Heavily feathered thighs.

SCAPULAR: Shoulder feathers.

MAXILLA: The top half of the bill.

MANDIBLE: The bottom half of the bill.

PASSSERINE: Perching birds.

PASSERIFORMES: perching birds.

GULAR POUCH: A loose sac or pouch of skin used to hold fish or inflated to draw attention in courtship displays. Other than Pelicans, only males have gular pouches.

DISPLAYING: Things the male does to gain attention of a mate during breeding season, puffing up a part of their body, changing colors, growing plentiful long feathers, besides the actions that are most frantic and include singing, dancing and running about excitedly as if staging a main event.

ECLIPSE: An annual preparation for the breeding season where feathers are shed and colors change completely in some cases, as well as patterns and habits. Colorful males become colorless and drab and change to their glorious colors again just before mating.

TARSI OR TARSUS: From the Greek word Tarsos: ankle. The leg of a bird. Note that the legs and feet or still scaled as once birds were scaled all over because they were reptiles before they began to fly. Feathers replaced scales.

TERMINALS & BARS: symetrical horizontal stripes or markings on the body or wings.

EVOLUTION OF BIRDS
(whose descendants are in this book)
UPPER JURASSIC
130 to 140 million years past
Archaeopteryx
(Ancient Bird)
1.Size of a crow
2.Well developed flight feathers
3.Claws at the bend of the wing
4.Teeth in the bill
5.Vertebrae extending into the tail

LOWER CRETACEOUS
110 to 120 million years past
Faint history of Water Fowl

UPPER CRETACEOUS
80-90 to 100 million years past
Waders & Gulls
Snowy Egret * Scarlet Ibis *
Wattled Jacana * Red Footed Booby
Little Blue Heron * Laughing Gull
Purple Gallinule * Roseate Spoonbill
Greater Flamingo * Least Sandpiper
Adult Least Bittern * White Ibis
Reddish Egret * Royal Tern
Common Tern * Anhinga
Dunlin * Brown Pelican
Frigate
PALEOCENE
70 million years past
EOCENE
50 to 60 million years past
Burrowing Owl * Marsh Harrier
Cascara * Red Tailed Hawk

EOCENE
50 to 60 million years past
Rufus Browed Peppershrike
Violaceous Euphonia
Pale Vented Pigeon
Blue Hooded Euphonia
Blue Crowned Motmot
Bay Headed Tanager
Common Ground dove
Silver Beaked Tanager
White Bearded Manakin
Stripe Headed Tanager
Blue Crowned Cholorophonia
White Crested Guan
Swallow Tailed Kite
Yellow Faced Grassquit
Swallow Tanager
Variable Seedeater

OLIGOCENE
30 to 40 million years past
Saffron Finch
Imperial parrot
Bee Hummingbird
Steamertail
Cuban Tody
Bananaquit
Red Legged Honeycreeper

MIOCENE
20 to 30 million years past

PLIOCENE
10 to 20 million years past
Tinamous

GENERALIZED BIRD CHARACTERISTICS

Our feathered friends have the strongest, warmest, most durable of all coverings, their feathers. They also have five pairs of air sacs throughout their bodies for bouyancy and respiration.

In order that a bird survive in its chosen habitat they must be equipped with adaptations that are best suited for their chosen homet at its most virulent nature. Most birds are clever enough to leave when their locale becomes untenable or unseasonable. Others , less fortuate, remain and may perish. Birds in southern climates have far reaching variances from birds in the Artic.

Every specie has at least four outstanding needs: the ability to find and obtain food, the ability to woo and win a mate for procreation and the ability to fight off predators to defend their lives and those of their offspring. Not many birds eat their young or the young of other birds, but some do with the absence of necessary and appropriate food. Survival is a primal and basic instinct.

Lastly birds need their natural assets to build their nests and the parental instincts that will aid and allow their young to survive birth and fledging at least. A bird's most important tools are its eyes, bill, talons and tail along with the ability to hold onto a perch and be able to take flight rapidly or to run and hide quickly.

Birds know innately about blending with their surroundings to hide from predators. Some perching birds lock their feet so they can sleep without falling from a branch, by locking the tendon in back of their heel and drawing their front toes tightly together to clamp onto the branch to sleep without falling. Even though their perch appears to be perilous, it is not.

Birds have super keen vision to allow for spotting prey from a great distance, Peregrine Falcons, Hawks and Eagles and Osprey not only have excellent eyesight but the added ability to focus quickly. Their quick head movements are described by humans as bird like and darting as if nervous in their movements. Some humans have the same high strung, quickly darting nature.

Birds are aided by the addition of an extra eyelid that is no more than a transparent membrane covering the eye, cleaning it, protecting it from glaring sunlight, and keeping it from watering when making deep underwater dives or when air rushes past the eye irritating it. Birds who have this membrane employ it for safety.

Unlike other members of the animal kingdom, most birds see colors vividly. That is the reason they are so gayly garbed and easily distinguishable from one another. It is believed that Hawks do not see all colors but definitly see variations in light and dark shades, especially regarding black and white. Certainly they see well enough to be one of the major aviary raptors.

In proportion to a bird's size, its eyes are remarkably large. When compared to its brain they are equal in size.

Depending on its habitat and the type of food it consumes, all birds are blessed with the right kind and size bill to retrieve life supporting food. Besides the bill, birds employ their tongues, wings, feet, body weight and tail to assist in their efforts to obtain food.

The Owl, Falcon, Hawk, Eagle, Osprey and Vulture all eat live or recently living birds or small rodents. These species more often snatch live prey in the air, and are equipped with very strong talons for gripping their prey. One puncture with these amazingly strong, agile talons can kill a bird or small creature immediately.

These species are also outfitted with particularly strong and sharp, hooked beaks to tear the flesh of their prey. These birds are good, inveterate hunters, often hunting at night when there is less traffic in the air. The shape and weight of these hunter species allows them to fly swiftly at a high altitudes, to dive on their prey from above and take them unaware.

These raptors land before devouring their prey, sometimes dropping the catch while planning their descent to eat their meal. They learn early, how to maneuver their wings and tails to direct or rapidly alter flight patterns.

Seed eating birds like Finch or Grosbeak, have short, strong, sharp beaks to enable them to get at the seeds inside a pine cone, embedded in bark, under natural objects or inside dry fruit or berries.

The Pelican has a large flexible pouch (gular) under its beak, suitable for catching many fish at once and storing them until they can eat them. Pelicans have the ability to rise into the air straight from the water carrying a load of many pounds of fish in their gular. Wading birds, stand for hours with their feet and ankles covered in mud or sand, searching shallow water for edible prey, that inevitably swims by. Their long bills are capable of spearing fish or picking them up and agilely slipping them down their long necks. They also eat the eggs of insects that are plentiful on bark or broad leaves, even in the water.

Ground feeding birds have short, stout bills suitable for pecking at the ground for nourishment left by larger birds, grain thrown by a keeper, or seeds that are released by a plant carried by the wind and land on earth or stone.

Many birds of this type spend half their day pecking at the ground for morsels. Their strong bills crush seeds easily.

Broad flat bills are used for straining nutrients and small morsels from underwater, sand or mud. Geese, ducks and long legged flamingos have proper bills for accessing their food. They literally shovel plants and small animal species into their bills and then sieve the water out the sides of their bills.

Ducks who eat fish have serrated edges to their bills to assist in catching and holding onto their prey. Their wide webbed feet propel them quickly through the water.

Loons and grebes nest in or at the edge of water. They dive for their food. Puffets and gannets nest on higher ground to more easily propel their bodies into the air when they spot their prey in the water from their high perch.

Warblers, Swallows and Swifts live primarily on insects and have slender pointed bills that facilitate the catching of any size insect. They troll in the air with their bills open, stuffing insects into their wide mouths. Otherwise they pick up insects or bugs crawling on leaves or branches. Birds are always looking for sustenance and spend much of their day hunting and eating .

Sandpipers and Snipes have long slender bills to probe flowers for nectar or to find morsels in sand or mud.

Long legged wading birds are blessed with long spreading toes that enable them to balance for hours on six inches of mud & gook.

They appear to be standing on water, patiently waiting for prey to swim close enough to snare.

All birds preen their feathers with their bills. The Heron has a toe with a comb that he uses to comb out his feathers and also to grip prey and crush it into small pieces.

Terns, doves and quail hang out at the sea shore and can be seen between the flow of the tide, running out on the tightly packed sand, shimmering with water and bubbles, looking for a telltale bubble that indicates a living critter beneath the surface of the sand. Here they employ their long slender bills to pierce the sand and perhaps snatch a morsel before running quickly back to high ground as the next wave sweeps over the sand.

The woodpecker uses his short straight bill like a hammer to pierce into a tree trunk with alacrity. Then he extends his strong muscled horney-tipped tongue through the hole he has created. The desired prey sticks to the tip of his tongue and he quickly withdraws his tongue to devour his morsel.

Due to a tendon that goes behind the bird's heel, and to secure his position vertically on the exterior of the tree, the woodpecker uses his two forward toes and his two backward toes as tongs, locking his feet in place, using the rear tendon to curl his front toes into a secure lock. Holding onto a tree, the woodpecker also secures his hold by using his tail feathers propped against the tree for a more secure hold.

Diving birds are wonderfully equipped for fast plunges into deep water. Their legs are set farther back on their bodies to make them better divers. This anomaly has to be compensated for on land because the bird's weight is greater in the front and balancing on their somewhat weak legs is much more difficult. Notice the fine erect posture, with these birds, which is a necessity that keeps them from losing their balance and toppling over.

With the exception of apes and monkeys most animals live in a monochronistic world, but not birds who see exquisite colors. The wildly colorful plumage of birds is much more important than just to thrill humans. Color combinations and design, the whole artistic display, in the fantastic world of birds plays a meaningful role in a bird's life, allowing males to sight females at a distance. Through color birds take notice of each other and are attracted, allowing for singular or group pride. They are in truly unique.

Strangely, certain birds choose only particular colors when selecting flower petals to line their nests. Obviously they know the full effect of colors. The inside of most chicks beaks are red. This color makes the parenting bird fetch more food to please their chicks for they are equally effected by red.

Females of most species are plain while the males are gloriously attired. Perhaps because the female has a major role in reproducing she does not need to attract by color or any means. It is enough that she is superior and extremely fulfilled.

Birds are attracted to each other's coloring just as they are attracted to bright lights that often dispel ultimate danger, especially when birds get trapped in the strong, captivating rays of gigantic flood lights and cannot break out of the powerful surge and continue to fly until their small hearts burst or they crash into objects or each other, and are knocked from the air and killed. This phenomenum is not unusual and sadly often repeated.

Sometimes it appears as if birds are in a panic and flying in circles. It takes a strong bird to lead the flock out of this impasse and break the cycle that has gripped them and led them in circles, especially if this happens in the middle of downtown automobile traffic particularly just before a storm. Birds have early sensor warning.

Like rats, some birds steal bright, shiny objects and surfeit them away in their nests. They will take things from a house especially if bright attractive items are left on window sills where birds like to land to survey the scene and maybe grab a bite of food. Birds enjoy the presence of light and these objects attract and reflect light. This gives the bird pleasure and is calming to them.

Blue is a color least easily recognized by birds, so insects would do well to bathe themselves in blue light, were that possible.

Hummingbirds beat their wings up to 75 times per second and hover to sip nectar from a flower. They can fly up and down, twist in the air and make tight, small turns and even spin backwards. Hummers are the only birds that can eat while literally flying.

TO THE BIRDS

A flash of brilliant hue
A movement quite sublime
A lilting song that lifts the heart
This is a bird

Of soaring flight
along airy paths
trailing in the sunlight
Our beloved creature

In deep verdant forests
high in canopied trees
resting beside a lily
sits a vibrant flier

Bathing in a fresh water puddle
shaking dew from its crown
stretching its legs, curling its toes
always cheerful, the bird

Hooting at the moon
In velvet darkness folded
cleaning the barn of rats
The barn owl does its duty

Startled by the lovely caged bird
Not knowing whether to pity or envy
Then flying on to fresher fields
An airborne spectator

Sitting on the hand of its owner
eating a piece of fruit
or sleeping on her shoulder
a human with its bird

by Lucy Baker

CARIBBEAN BIRD HABITATS

TROPICAL RAIN FORESTS

With an overhead canopy of large trees to attract rain and keep the forest cool, moist and humid. Air plants and lichens hang from branches. There is abundant low foliage, berries, seeds, vines, ferns, variegated leaves and flowers.

SWAMP FOREST

Wet or watery ground, sustaining large trees heavy with moss and herbaceous growth. Trees of many varieties, shrubs, bushes and thick ground cover. High humidity, heavy with insects and mosquitoes buzzing. Many species roost in surrounding trees, close to their food source.

SEMI-DECIDUOUS FOREST

Containing trees that lose their leaves annually, along with pines and non-deciduous trees that may grow to towering heights and are fragrant and have thick bark and bear cones and perhaps exotic flowers.

MANGROVE SWAMP

Ocean fed, thick, muddy, brackish water, often herbaceous, with floating leaves and fowers and heavy topped mangrove trees that are well adapted to growing in deep water and put out thick vine like roots that attach themselves in deep mud.

MANGROVE MARSHES

Brackish water: fresh mixed with salt, surrounded by tall grass, Pussywillows, Sawgrass, Floating Lilies, Hyacinths. Muddy bottom steaming with algae. Mangroves thick low umbrella growth, the perfect habitat for nesting birds

WETLANDS

Coastal ponds and mud flats usualy brackish, mangroves, shallow esturies, lagoons, salinas, herbaceous swamps and swamp forests.

FRESH WATER MARSHES OR SAVANNAS

Bodies of spring or rain fed water in valleys or plains surrounded by hills, montanes and mountains with lovely vistas, usually within sight of the sea.

SMALL PONDS AND LAGOONS

Near the sea or just inland, fed by the sea, fresh water springs or rain water. Often stagnant, polluted and brackish.
More dangerous to the health of humans than to animals, fowls and birds.

COASTAL

Shoreline and surf with beaches or cliffs, unihabited or isolated. Where large bodies of fish congregate and are easily plucked from the sea by clever, ever present sea birds.

COASTAL THICKET

Further inland, with more vegetation, grasses,bushes, shrubs and tall trees,flowers and less wind. Very little interference from large sea predators. Foliage often bent by the ever prevailing sea winds.

DRY LIMESTONE FORESTS

On the coastal plains and lower hills with scrubby growth, spindly trees, cleared land, unsheltered areas with cacti and thatch palms, and thorny species. Thick vines, rocks and boulders.

WET LIMESTONE FORESTS

Layered forest growth. Trees from 15 to 65 feet.
Shrubs and herbs,vines and bromeliads. Dark rich earth with fern species, orchids and air plants requiring shade,indirect light and coolness

MONTANE

Deep verdant valleys with lush growth, tall trees with bromeliads and ferns. Dark, dense and cool. Orchids, creepers moss and fungi. Strands of gray lichen traiing from trees. Overhead canopy of tall trees, sub-canopy of smaller varieties.

CULTIVATED LAND

Pastures sown with seed or seedlings distributed by birds. Ground vegetation, contiguous to cattle ponds, sometimes brackish but acceptable to cattle. Vegetable and planted flower gardens tended daily by humans.

RUGGED SEACLIFFS

Scrubby growth, stunted trees, bent over permanently. Tallgrasses, flowering weeds and perennial flowers. Rocky precipices and high platforms for stalking and roosting as well as caves for nesting.

DRY SCRUB WOODLAND

Sparse growth, many insects and creatures living in burrows and holes underground, by roadside embankments.

CORAL CAYS

Off shore islands formed by coral outcroppings, teeming with varieties of coral. An excellent home for aquatic life and many species of migrating birds looking for morsels of sustenance.

CLOUD FORESTS

Mooountain tops, above the rain forest and Palm breakers. Stunted, gnarled trees hanging bowers, fewer shrubs. Cool and moist mornings and evenings. Above 5000 feet, the Elfin Woodlands are shrouded in morning mist.

THE VENTASTEGA CURONICA

When a 365 million-year-old fossil was discovered in Latvia in 2008, it was hoped that a more defining evolutionary link had been established between fish and tetrapods. An earlier discovery had appeared to be more of a fish. This specimen is clearly a tetrapod.

Tetrapods have four limbs and are the forerunners of all amphibians, birds and mammals.

Only the scull, shoulders and parts of the pelvis were intact, leading authorities to believe that this creature had stubby limbs, perhaps with digits but these have not been found or confirmed.

This was a nasty looking creature who stalked fish in shallow water for sustenance.

Clearly outfitted for land or sea, the Ventastega was up to four feet long and most likely had scales on part if not most of its body.

As life began in the sea,this early tetrapod shows the development of four limbs for walking.

Later this would amorph to two limbs for some creatures and eventually the scales would turn to feathers and the long spinal column would eventually end at the body of the animal as they do today.

Note the obvious reptilian shape and design of the head and teeth lined jaw.

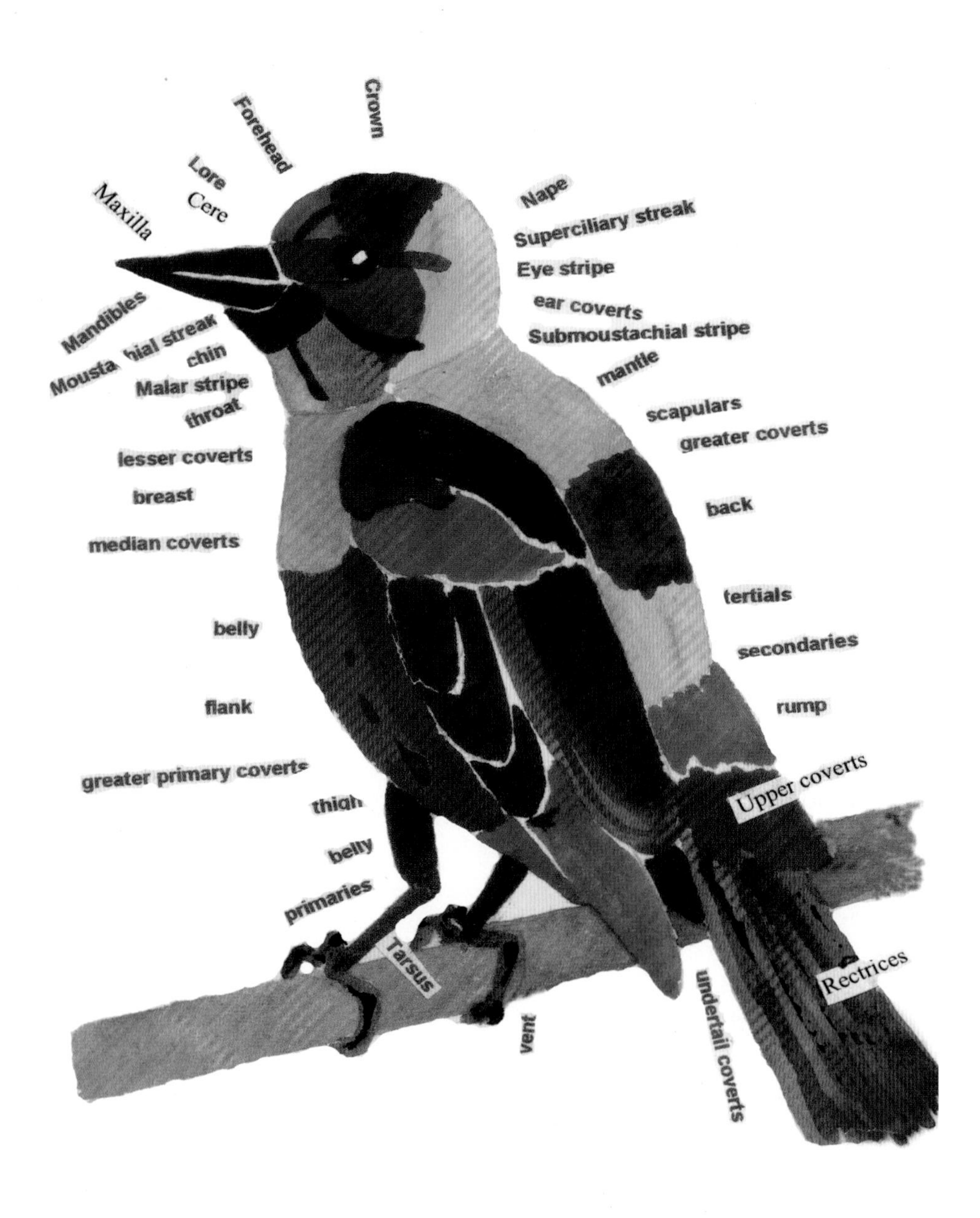
Crown
Forehead
Lore
Cere
Maxilla
Nape
Superciliary streak
Eye stripe
ear coverts
Submoustachial stripe
mantle
Mandibles
chin
Malar stripe
throat
scapulars
greater coverts
lesser coverts
breast
back
median coverts
tertials
belly
secondaries
flank
rump
Upper coverts
belly
primaries
Tarsus
Rectrices
vent
undertail coverts

THESE BIRDS ARE FOUND IN FRENCH OR DUTCH ST. MAARTEN IN THE LESSER ANTILLES, ST. EUSTTIUS, ST. BARTH'S, ST. KITT'S, NEVIS, ANGUILLA AND SABA

Some are migratory, others live, breed and nest on these islands, while some are ocasional visitors that are migrating further south.

IBISES & SPOONBILLS
Roseate Soonbill (rare)

SWANS, GEESE & DUCKS
White Cheeked Pintail (rare)
Northern Pintail
American Wigeon
Lesser Scaup

SHEARWATERS & PETRELS
Audubon's Shearwater

STORM PETRELS
Wulson's Storm Petrel
Leach's Storm Petrel
White-tailed Tropicbirdl
Red-billed Tropicbird

PELICANS
Brown Pelican

CORMORANTS
Double-crested Cormorants (rare)

FRIGATE BIRDS
Magnificent Frigate bird

OWLS
Short-eared Owl

WOODCOCK & SNIPE &
Greater Yellowlegs
Willet
Whimbrel
Ruddy Tumstone

PLOVERS & TURNSTONES
Semi-palmated Plover

AVOCETS & STILTS
Black-necked Stilt

SANDPIPERS & SNIPES
Spotted Sandpiper
Solitary Sandpiper
Semipalmated Sandpiper
Western Sandpiper
Least Sandpiper
Stilt Sandpiper
Short-billed Dowicher
Common Sniper
Artic Skua

CARDINALS & GROSBEAKS
Streaked Saltator
Indigo Bunting

GULLS & TERNS
Laughing Gull
Ring-billed Gull
Herring Gull
Lesser Black-backed Gull
Great Black-backed Gull
Gull-billed Tern
Royal Tern
Sandwich Tern
Roseate Tern
Common Tern
Least Tern
Brown Noddy

Bridled Tern
Sooty Tern
Black Noddy
Common Tern
Least Tern
Bridled Tern
Sooty Tern
Brown Noddy
Black Noddy

TYRANT FLYCATCHERS
Lesser Antillean Fycatcher
Gray Kingbird

BANANAQUITS
Bananaquits, “Sugar Bird”

SWALLOWS
Caribbean Martin
Ciff Swallow
Indigo Bunting
Barn Swallow

MUSCICAPIDS, SOLITARES & THRUSHES
Veery

MOCKNGBIRDS & THRASHERS
Scaly-breasted Thrasher
Pearly-eyed Thrasher
Trembler

VIREOS
Black-whiskered Vireo

EMEDERIZIDS
Northern Parula Warbler
Yellow Warbler
Cape May Warbler
Black-throated Blue Warbler
Prairie Warbler

EMEDERIZIDS (cont.)
Blackpoll Warbler
Black & White Warbler
American Redstart
Prothonary Warbler
Ovenbird
Northern Waterbrush
Louisiana Waterbrush
Hooded Warbler

RAILS, GALLINULES & COOTS
Sora
Purple Gallinule
Common Moorhen
American Coot
Caribbean Coot

PIGEONS & DOVES
Scaly-naped or red-necked Pigeon
White Crowned Pigeon
Zenaida Dove
Grenada Dove
Bridled Quail Dove

COOKOOS & ANIS
Yellow-billed Cuckoo
Mangrove Cuckoo
Smooth-billed Ani

NIGHTJARS
Common Night Hawk
Antilean Nighthawk
Chuck-will's widow

SWIFTS
Black Swift
White-collared Swift

HUMMINGBIRDS
Purple-throated Carib
Green-throated Carib
Antillean Crested Hummiingbird

KINGFISHERS
Belted Kingfisher

PICULETS & WRYNECKS
Yellow-bellied Sapsucker

TYRANT FLYCATHERS
Caribbean Elaenia
Lesser Antillean Pewee
Red Knot
Sanderling

BOOBIES & GANNETS
Brown Booby

HERONS & BITTERNS
Great Blue Hero
Great Egret
Snowy Egret
Green Backed Heron
Yellow Crowned Night Heron
Little Blue Heron
Tricolored Heron
Cattle Egret
GLosssy Ibis (rare)

OSPREYS
Osprey

GREBES
Pied-billed Grebe

CARIBBEAN PLANT FOOD FOR BIRDS

Ackee	Indian Corn	Bamboo
Jamaican Mistletoe	Bitterwood	Logwood
Blud mahoe	Mangrove, black	Bouganvillea
Button,red&whte	Broadleaf	Maiden Plum
Bromeliads	Maypole	Broughtonia
Mountain Pride	Bullet	Naseberry
Burnwood	Oncidium	Cashaw
Orange	Casuarina	Peach
Chinese Hat	Pentas	Cho-Cho
Peppers	Coconut	Pimento
Coffee	Pine Trees	Erythrna
Plaintain	Fiddlewood	Poincianna
French peanut	Poison Sumac	Ginger Lilies
Prickly Pear	Guava	Privet
Guinea Grass	Pudding White	Hibicus
Red Birch	Royal Palm	Santa Maria
Soursop	Spanish Moss	Spanish Ganja
Spanish Needle	Spathodea	Strangler Fig
Sweetwoods	Tamarind	Thatch Palms
Tree Ferns	Trupet Tree	Vervain
Vines	Waxwood	West Indian Cedar
Wild Bauhinia (Bullhoof		yacca

ARCHAEOPTERYX: ANCIENT BIRD
(Lucy Baker's idea of the prototype)

Fossil like remains found in Bavaria confirm that 130 million years ago there was a flying reptilian type, the size of a crow, descendant of an upright dinosaur with teeth in its bill, claws at the bend in the wings and a vertebrated tail. Their breastbone being immaturey developed indicates that they were poor flyers.

INTRODUCTION

Other then mankind, birds are the most interesting and unusual of God's creations. Think about the wonderful way they look and the fact that they can fly and sing and take care of themselves through every kind of adversity and the pleasure they bring to humans and what our world would be like without these marvelous creatures.

Birds sing, some beautifully, and they dance, some quite imaginatively, and they are incredibly funny and amusing, some seemingly born comediens. Lastly, and most amazing, they can fly with style and elegance and are breathtakingly beautiful, others can fly great distances, even around the world without stopping for food or water. Some take flight against danger, some fly while sipping nectar, others carry messages for humans and many fly for safeties sake and to ease the toil of their daily living. This is called migration and has gone on through the centuries with birds returning to the same places generation after generation. Here they might winter in comfort and ease before returning to their true habitation to breed. Where a bird breeds is their habitat.

Birds solve problems instinctively, being more trusting than man. It is as if birds know their creator better than mankind may.

Birds do something marvelous for mankind by making us feel comfortable with nature. By their example we learn from them. In understanding them we better understand our selves and our path and therefore better accept our role in the universe.

Due to our individuality we are attracted to specific types of birds, according to our own nature. Serious men are not impressed with cute little birds that sit on a perch all day and sing. Whereas they may find a falcon, hawk, osprey or harrier excited and stiimulatiing. A ballet dancer and artist is thrilled by the colorful, elegant and numerous graceful moves of birds in flight. Students and scholors might remark on the highly ethical owl or hard working tanagers. Mild natured women and men may admire the gentle dove and a circus clown would envy the toucan. There is something admirable about every single bird, for each has a purpose and struggles to be fulfilled. Most of them work very hard.

With mankind at the top of the species on earth, we have an added responsibility to see that all species are treated fairly. There are those who believe that eagles who are at the top of the bird kingdom, have the possibility of tranmigrating into humans. Their counterpart in the oceans, the dolphin, is also elligible to become human.

Certainly humans are bonded with birds. We admire them and they brighten our lives.

Birds belong to the class called "Ave," meaning they are vertebrates: having a spine and a bony skeleton and are covered with feathers. Feathers are a valuable aide, they keep the bird's body warm and waterproofed.

Birds share a common link with amphibians that crawled, scampered and dragged themselves out of the slime of the Paleozoic age over 300 million years ago; the beginning of life on earth. From that beginning their evolution is traced.

With advantages, some specimens developed more easily into reptilian species. Their next evolution was into two footed creatures, while some needed and retained four feet. It was almost as if certain species decided not to evolve to two feet and were happy remaining as they were. We do not know if these stubborn creatures continued to evolve. It seems that those that do not participate in constant evoution are destined to die out.

According to available food, if they had to eat each other or exist on plants, and how many predators were afoot and if the opposite sex was handy for breeding, this determined whether a particular species would survive or needed to make a complete life change, (necessary adaptation).

The life force was and is so strong that had all of earth's great oceans and seas dried up, the creatures living in the water would have adapted to land. Likewise, had all plants died, those eating them would have found another food, maybe even resorting to eating each other. No one supposes the dinosaurs suffered from ethics when they gobbled down their enemy's young or each other. As in the jungle,many animals survive by devouring other animals and are not considered murderers.

INDEX OF BIRDS

1.	Anhinga:	Anhinga anhinga
2.	Bananaquit	Coeraba flaveola
3.	Bay-headed Tanager	Tangara gyrola
4.	Bee Hummingbird	Calypte helenae
5.	Belted Kingfisher	Megaceryle alcyon
6.	Black-Headed Saltator	Saltator atriceps
7.	Blue Diademed MotMot	Momotus momota
8.	Blue Crowned Chlorphonia	occipitali
9.	Brown Pelican	Pelecanus occidentalis
10.	Burrowing Owl	Speolyto cunicularia
11.	Caracara	Caracara Cheriway
12.	Channel-billed Toucan	Ramphastos vitellinus
13.	Common Ground Do	Columbina passerina
14.	Common Tern	Sterna hirundo
15.	Crested Tinamou	Eudromia elegans
16.	Cuban Tody	Pedorrera carticuba
17.	Dunlin	Calidris alpina
18.	Gartered Trogan	Trogan violaceus
19.	Gray-headed Quail	Coquito banc
20.	Greater Flamingo	Phoenicopterus reber
21.	Green Honeycreeper	Chlorophanes spiza
22.	Imperial Parrot	Amazonia imperialis
23	Jamaican Mango	Anthracithirax mango
24.	Laughing Gull	Larus atricilla
25.	Least Bittern	Ixobrychus exilis
26.	Least Sandpiper	Calidris minutillia
27.	Little Blue Heron	Hydranass caerules
28.	Male Frigate (displaying	Pelicaniformes Fregatidae
29.	Marsh Harrier	Circus cyaneus
30.	Pale Vented Pigeon	Patagioenas cayennensis
31.	Passerinis Tanager	Ramphocelus paserinii

32.	Peregrine Falcon	Falco peregrinus
34.	Purple Gallinule	Porphyrula martinica
35.	Red Footed Booby	Sula sula
36.	Red Legged Honeycreeper	Cyanerpes cyanueus azulito
37.	Red Tailed Hawk	Buteo jamaicensis
38.	Red Billed Streamertail	Trochilus polytmus
39.	Reddish Egret	Egretta rufescens
40.	Roseatte Spoonbill	Ajaja ajaja
41.	Royal Tern	Thalesseus maximus
42.	Rufous Browed Peppershrike	Cyclarhis gujanensis
43.	Saffron Finch	Sicalis flaveola
44.	Scarlet Ibis	Eudocimus ruber
45.	Silver Beaked Tanager	Ramphocelus carbo
46.	Snowy Egret	Egretta thula
47.	Spectacled Owl	Pulsatrix perspicillata
48.	Swallow Tailed Kite	Elanoides forficatus
49.	Swallow Tanager	Tersina viridis
50.	Veritable Seedeater	Sorophila aurita
51.	Violaceous Euphonia	Euphonia violacea
52.	Wattled Jacana	Jacana jacana
53.	Western Spindalis	Spindalis zena
54.	White Bearded Manakin	Manacus manacus
55.	White Crested Guan	Penelope purpurascens
56.	White Ibis	Eudocimus albus
57.	Yellow Faced Grassquit	Tiaris olivaceus

(111 color images)

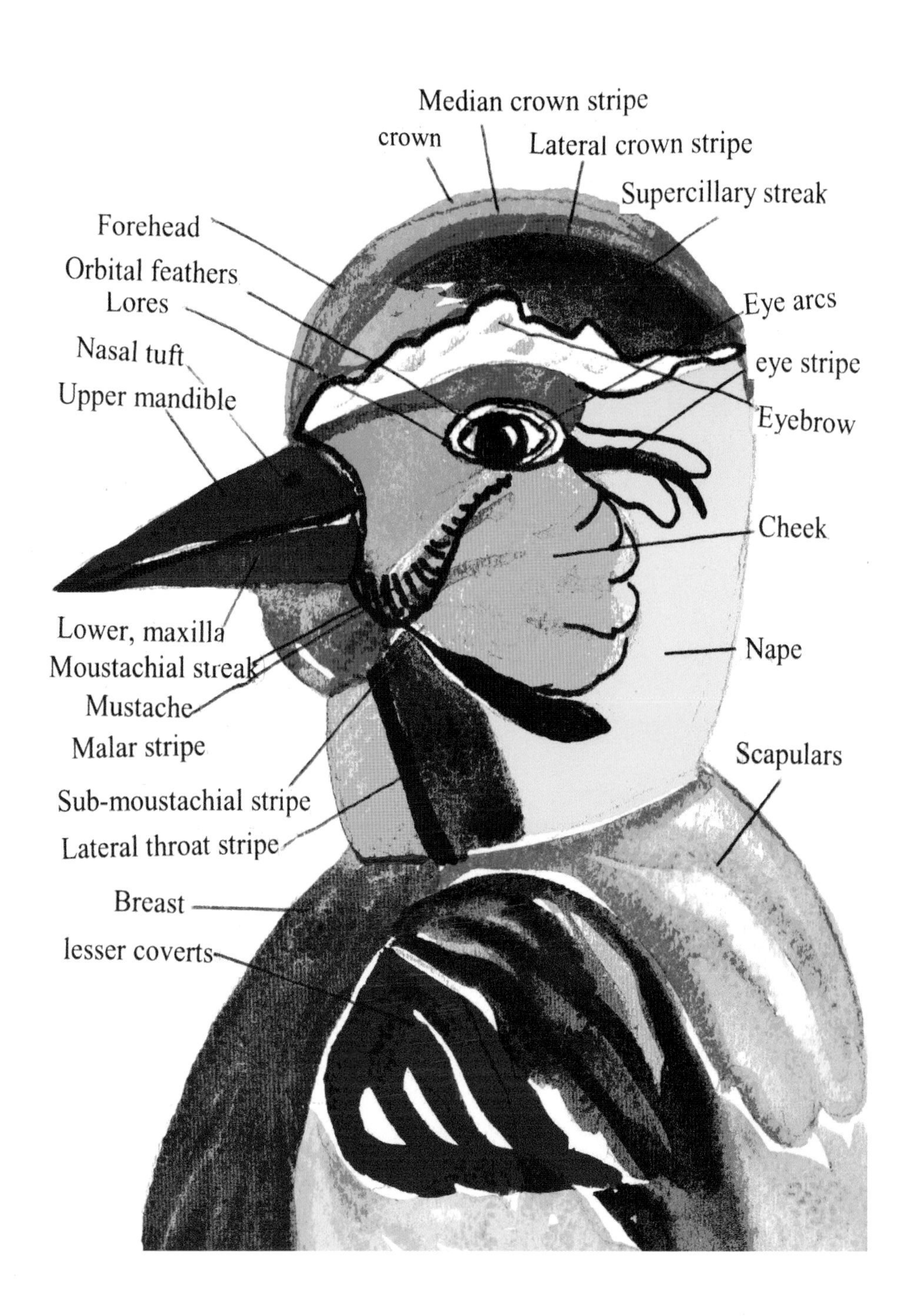

Median crown stripe
crown
Lateral crown stripe
Supercillary streak
Forehead
Orbital feathers
Lores
Eye arcs
Nasal tuft
eye stripe
Upper mandible
Eyebrow
Cheek
Lower, maxilla
Moustachial streak
Nape
Mustache
Malar stripe
Scapulars
Sub-moustachial stripe
Lateral throat stripe
Breast
lesser coverts

ANHINGA

Scientific Name: Anhinga anhinga
Common Name: Snakebird or Water turkey
Family:Anhingidae (darters)
Order: Pelicaniformes
Length: 32 to 36 inches

On the planet for 80 million years, Eocene fossils have been found to prove their antiquity. A relative of the cormorant, except that unlike the cormorant the Anhinga avoids salt or brackish water.

The Anhinga's thickly packed furry plumage is a glossy greenish black with pale gray layered wing coverts of irregular lengths. The female's head, neck and breast are a pale whitish gray.

The bones of this large and unusual bird are heavy and capable of real strength. This is a distinct aid in the steep dives the Anhinga makes to catch prey.

This bird's external nostrils are always closed, a necessity in its constant diving and venturing into the sea. The addition of a strange hair lined stomach strains fish bones that might otherwise kill the bird for they cannot digest this matter and must evacuate it through other means than processed through their bodies so they regurgitate these bits of bone.

Anhingas live in fresh water sloughs, ponds and bayous or in shallow river beds in temperate or tropical climates where there are small bushes and low growing trees in which they sit holding their wings wide, warming and drying them in the sun, a necessity for such a thick, almost mat like growth of feathers that are easily saturated with water and oil and grow too heavy for the bird to be able to fly.

Their nests have been found as high as thirty feet, a cautious and safe area as long as the chicks are carefully attended to so high off the ground.

The Anhinga lays three to six chalky, bluish white eggs that are pointed on one end, between March and May, or even as late as July. The nest is always in a tree The eggs take about 28 days to hatch.

The male and female take turns feeding the chicks by regurgitating food into their gullets. Chicks are born bare and blind but are soon covered in white fleecy down. They remain in the nest for 8 weeks and then instinctively go directly into the water, a natural habitat for them.

The parents enjoy long steady and high flights above their nest, soaring in large circles as if for amusement. They are graceful only in flight and seem to enjoy flying.

The water is where they feed and hide from predators. Occasionally their worst enemies are also in the water, waiting to snare them, kill them and eat them.

The Anhinga is called the snakebird because they swim with their long neck floating on top of the water looking much like a snake to fool predators.

They are called darters because they use their coiled neck to strike prey quickly with a darting motion. If there are no fish, the Anhinga eats frogs, salamanders, crayfish and insects.

If a victim flays and fights to get free, the Anhinga beats it against the rocks or shakes it to subdue it before devouring it. Anhingas keep company with herons and ibises and often make their nests in mixed colonies. Usually silent, they can click and rattle when they want to within this company of friends.

BANANAQUIT

Coereba flaveola

(Banana bird: Sugar Bird)

Length: 4 to 5 inches

The Bananaquit varies in appearance and habit according to its geographical habitat. The Banaquit is one of 35 sub-species.

A member of the warbler family, Banaquits are small, dainty birds. When molting they are drab and dull, but decked out for spring and breeding they are beautiful in bright yellow, blue and red, absolutely cheerful and so sassy that everyone who sees them is delighted.

This is a nectar eating bird with a thin pointed bill for probing flower stamens. The Bananquit pierces the base of the flower to inbibe more easily.

These birds are not strong singers. Their frustrating but noble efforts sound like buzzing or lisping. Each bird creates its own song. One common call is: zee-e-e-e-e sweeste, another gives a high pitched tumbling trill followed by mechanical clicking like a wind up toy.

Banaquits are found in the company of humans, seeking sweets and treats, always begging. They fly into your house, land on your table, and aim for the sugar bowl. Then nonchalantly join you in a meal. They know where the exit is. Flying through the house they are charming. Occasionally they will light on a rafter. They never roost low and remain cautious except where sweets are concerned

Unless they have established a nest of their own, they will use any nest conveniently at hand.

Bananaquits nest once a year and build a bulky domed nest with a side entrance near the bottom, where the female lays three white eggs speckled with brown. Nest building is done by the male but the female lines the nest with soft leaves in a thicket on the ground. She will incubate the eggs for two weeks until they hatch.

The male builds several nests nearby to be close to the main nest. He brings the female food while she is incubating. Nestling takes another two weeks with the female alone with the fledglings with no male in sight.

Migratory flights begin in good weather, often at night, but often end in chaos with thousands of birds dead from the perils they have encountered. Bad weather and intensely bright beams from lighthouses or airports are their biggest problem. Caught in the brightness of these beams, the birds cannot escape and circle until they crash into each other or surrounding walls, or fall dead from exhaustion. This kind of tragedy has effected the population quite drastically

The Banaquit's habitat in the entire Caribbean with the exception of Cuba, and they certainly are not political. They have widespread presence in Central and So. America and are also found in the Bahamas and West Indies.

The Banaquit is quick and flighty, easily stirred up and ready to fly away quickly. They remain friendly if skittish, often amuzed and a total delight to tourists who love to have the birds eating sugar at their table.

Banaquits eat insects in large numbers alone, or with a partner. They do not congregate in flocks and they hate bananas but love other fruits including sapodillas.

This specie is not threatened at this time.

BAY HEADED TANAGER

Tangara gyrola

Length: 5 ½ inches

There are nine sub-species of tanagers.

This most common of all three forest tanagers are well known on Trinidad where they frequent the forest area and bushy thickets. They prefer to live in montanes: a zone of relatively moist, cool upland slopes below the timberline dominated by large coniferous trees, or in the foothills, a canopy of forested habitats, or on the edge of agricultural plantations. They particularly enjoy the cottonwood and sycamore trees where they sing, eat and socialize.

Being neo-tropical migrants, migrating from North America they head to the southern locations for sun and warmth and for their joyful annual breeding.

The Bay-Headed Tanager is found in the northern mountains at higher altitudes. They do not mind cool but absolutely require moist forests.

The Bay-Headed Tanager also inhabits Costa Rica, Panama, South America, Ecuador, Brazil & Bolivia.

The tanager is socially inclined and friendly to humans and other birds. He is called acrobatic due to his quick and amusing stunts.

Bay-headed Tanagers are sexually dimorphic, the female being the same size and coloration.

Both the female and male are brightly decked with gorgeous plumage; in shades of green with a chestnut cap and a blue belly. They have a thin gold collar around the back of their neck. Only mature birds wear the red cap. The young birds are duller and their green heads are flecked with chestnut shapes that change to a solid color when

they mature. This happens after at least the first year.

Their frequent call may be a slow, soft twittering: "seeee,seeee,seeee,tsouuu, tsooyy," or it may be a sharp, metallic single ear-piercing note. Depending on their mood they are either garnering attention or showing off.

Tanagers feed on every kind of nut available in their habitat. They have tried many and have their favorites.

In the spring they eat insects that are plentiful and by summer switch to the fruit that has just ripened. They eat all types of ripe berries and multiple small fruits growing on cultivated or wild vines, trees or bushes.

The tanager will eat epiphytes, the small plants that grow on other plant leaves supported by the moisture produced by rain, air and the nutrients that are on the surface of the plant to which they harmlessly attach.

Tanagers seek the insects that run up and down tree branches on their own quest for food.

These birds are known to eat small fruits whole. The tanager forages consistently for live prey in areas known to have plentiful insects.

Tanagers create an unusually fine cup nest out of moss that is unique to their breed and both beautiful and utilitarian. They appear to be very proud of their efforts.

The tanager supports this nest by connecting it securely to the fork of a tree and fastening both sides to opposite branches, being sure it will hold fast.

Their clutch contains two white eggs with blotchy brown markings, which the female incubates alone.

After the chicks are hatched,the male usually comes in to help obtain food for the mother and the chicks. This specie is considered good at parenting.

BEE HUMMINGBIRD

Calypte helenae

Length: 2 ¼ inches

Boldly iridescent in a diminutive size, these birds are as delightful as a sparkling jewel, the smallest of the family of Hummingbirds, the likely descendants of tropical Swifts. Hummers range south to South America, north to Quebec and Nova Scotia and are plentiful in the West Indies.

Living almost solely on nectar, this tiny bird extends its tongue beyond its bill to suck nectar.

Their wings beat so fast, (sixty miles an hour) that they hum, hence their nic-name.

Hummers feet are weak and small. Consequently they scracely ever walk and will fly even inches although they migrate 500 miles without stopping. First they load up with food fuel, increasing their body weight by 50% before beginning their long, planned flight.

Their metabolism drops perceptibly at night, to conserve energy.

Being duirnal, their temperature rises daily with the intake of nectar and energy is immediately restored.

Hummers eat the insects in flowers, and forage in spider's nests for prey thereby doing effective cross-pollination, accidently carrying pollen on and around their heads from flower stamen to flower stamen.

They move at lightning speed, up and down, sideways and backwards with equal and amazing agility.

This is the only bird that can hover above its food and eat while flying.

They have been taught to drink out of a small glass vial held by a human.

BELTED KINGFISHER

Megaceryle alcyon

Length: 13 inches

The belted kingfisher is a migratory bird that breeds in North America and migrates south to Central American and South America throughout the winter. They are found year round in the West Indies with other kingfishers who have not taken to migrating.

TheBelted Kingfisher's line extends back to the ice age. They live all over the world except in the artic.

Kingfishers have plump bodies, short necks, large heads with a blue erectile crest. Their tails are short & stubby. Their bills are strong and end in a spear point. Their legs are short and their feet small and weak. Their front toes are joined like webbed toes makaing it impractical to build nests or dig. Kingfishers are beautiful in blue and white with patches of barred red, and dramatic spotting in white. The female is distinguishable from the male by her double banded breast bars, one rufous, one gray. The male has a gray band across his chest.

Often found in Jamaica and Tobago they add their raucous excitement to the surrounding cacophony.

They favor swampy land, reservoirs, rivers, lakes, lagoons and fresh water streams or coastal plains where they feast on a bounty of aquatic fish and insects. In a shortage of minnows the kingfisher switches to other species, including crustaceans and reptiles.

Oddly in the winter they visit salty, brackish watering holes, perhaps out of curiosity. Their bills are powerful and dagger shaped and they often employ stealth in stalking their prey by leaning over the water hanging onto a branch.

From this perch they are able to dart down and snatch a passing fish or any variety of marine life. Plunging in for a quick grab, they return to land to kill and devour their prey, which they swallow head first. They also hover 20 feet above water and dive in to spear a fish. They may pound a crayfish with their strong bill, crushing it so it will be tender enough to eat.

They make their nests in deep holes burrowed into muddy banks of streams and lakes, safe from the pull of a rising and receding tide.

Using their long beaks and partially joined toes,they create a tunnel by digging 3 to 10 feet into a bank, ending in a round chamber where the female lays 8 white eggs directly on the dirt floor. The burrow soon becomes littered with bits of food and debris brought in by the adults who are extremely messy and live in their garbage.

The parents take turns incubating the eggs for at least 24 days. The chicks hatch naked and blind but develop quickly. They remain in the burrow until they sprout feathers, about four weeks. After the fledglings leave the nest the parents stay with them and feed them until the young are capable of fishing for themselves. Adults breed twice a year in the tropics, aided by the warm weather.

Kingfishers fly by quick wing beats and then glide on the prevailing currents and simply repeat this pattern, Except when migrating they follow waterways, always flying within sight of the water for assurance.

Kingfishers are not good singers. Their calls in flight sound like a series of rattles, similar to the awful noise made by New Year's eve sound makers;not a pretty sound but sure to attract attention.

BLACK-HEADED SALTATOR

Saltator atriceps

Order: Passiformes Family: Fringillidae

Length: 10 inches

Saltator is the name for a large bird that closely resembles the sparrow or finch in appearance, but is much larger. The members of this family number 690 species. Fringillidae being one of the largest families in the entire kingdom of flying creatures we call birds.

The Saltator lives in Central and South America along with Mexico as well as the Caribbean islands. Their behavior is mannerly and subdued. They do not fuss and never argue. This variety is the largest bird in his genus but he is as kind and polite as a gentleman.

Their favorite habitat is open woodlands at the edge of great forests where land is cleared for cultivation. They also like wide grassy fields where tall, slim grasses blow in soft enchanted breezes.

The Saltator has a black head with large arching white eyebrows over white lores marked with black etchings around red orbitals surrounded by a black eye ring.

These birds have white pointed ceres above a grey and black pointed long, sharp convex bill that looks like a finche's but is not as stout. It's feet are brown. Its thighs are grey and its legs are yellowish brown. Its tail feathers are long and yellow with black markings as are its median, greater, primary and tertial coverts and its secondary wings and upper tail coverts. He is well edged all over.

There are bluish white markings on its breast and below its belly they have light colors. Their vent is white as seen from the ground when they are in flight.

Saltators love the humidity of the tropics and are happiest in temperate zones. They cannot live without warmth and moisture.

Their diet consists of flower petals, fruits and berries although they are considered seed eaters and do eat certain seeds, for seeds are not their favorite food.
Saltators feed in flocks at their whim.

Like most tanagers, the Black headed Saltator's voice is dissapointingly raucous and weak for so large a bird with a full breast. He sings, "chair, chair, jewey, jewey, weeeee." One of his single calls might sound like he is calling dearie in a loud and nasty voice. Fortunately they do not often call and never sing although males will attempt to harmonize with each other as though they are experimenting.

The sexes are very much alike in appearance, (dimorphic). During breeding season the male attracts a female by any subtrafuge available, they may mate any time between April and July.

The female builds a grass lined cup nest in a thicket while the male stands by watching and waiting to see if he is needed.

Here in her neat little nest, the female lays 2 pale blue eggs and incubates them for two weeks. After the chicks hatch the male come to help feed the chicks and the female, if necessary.

Even after the chicks have fledged but are still staying close to the nest or in it, the parents continue to feed them. This may continue for two weeks to give the young a perfect start in life.

Few birds are as examplary as the Black headed Saltator's whose parenting skills are outstanding.

BLUE DIADEMED MOTMOT

Momotus momota (Jacamars)

Length: 18 inches

This beautiful bird has remarkable & unique racquet tipped tails, that are short, naked & slender shafts ending with a broad feather at each end. In flight these tails rub together to make a loud rattling sound. Eight species of these long tailed birds range from Mexico to Argentina and are found living on Trinidad, Tobago and Costa Rico.

Motmots often hide, even though they are not shy, especially in forests, for they are easily located and can be watched unaware for hours.

They cohabit in pairs that remain together all year, sweetly calling to each other during the day and at twilight. The exception are Mot Mots who prefer to be alone except for the annual breeding season.

This bird perches on a low limb for hours, on the look out for food that may come near him; watching humans or animals while twitching their long odd, fancy tails from side to side for some odd reason.

Their feathers are soft and pretty in colorful shades of subdued green. They have a brightly marked face in blue with a bright blue crown. They wear a dramatic black mask that partly covers the crown, surrounds the lores and extends midway around the bird's head. A dramatic blazing red shield covers their breast.

Their deep yellow beaks are broad and large, shaped in a gentle downward curve with serrated inner edges to assist in ripping their food. They eat beetles, grasshoppers, spiders and large insects.

Their eyes are a bright, deep golden yellow ringed in

black and their vision is excellent.

Their diet is comprised of lizards, frogs, snails, and they eat beetles, grasshoppers, spiders and large insects as well.

Their eyes are a bright, deep golden yellow ringed in black, and their vision is excellent.

If their prey is large or tough they pound it until it breaks up and then eat it in small pieces.

Motmots roost on public wires and windows of buildings and under eaves, or they cling to branches in fairly low trees in public parks, where they can easily be spotted.

They exist in well-populated areas abundant with rough, ill behaving boys, dogs and cats, and the adults who abuse them. Still, they like contact with humans, and the morsels that humans dispense.

In Trinidad and Tobago the Motmot is called "King of the Woods." The Motmot makes a muffled, resinous hooting call. They can handle larger prey like reptiles, birds and a variety of invertebrates that they beat on the rocks to tenderize. They are fond of fruit and will eat from your hand.

Motmots lay 3 oval white eggs in crevices or in a tunnel 6 inches long burrowed in a sloping channel in a muddy river bank that ends in a rounded chamber where the eggs are laid on the ground.

Both sexes incubate the eggs for 21 days and rear the fledglings for 4 to 5 weeks together until their feathers come in and they have become fledglings. The young depart before their wing and tail feathers have filled out or their bills are developed with the necessary serrations.

Motmots create a filthy tunnel chamber, thick with droppings and bits of spoiled food that they never clean up. and would obviously rather leave and forget.

BLUE-CROWNED CHLOROPHONIA

Chlorophonia occipitalis (Mistletoe bird)

Length: 4 ¾ inches

One of four migrant species of the New World tanagers, the euphonia differs from the other tanagers in that the females are colored differently from their male counterparts. Gay year round colors are the hallmark of these brilliant, velvety tanagers.

This short, round, almost dumpy bird is under five inches and has a short tail and a short stubby bill.

Males are always distinctly green, blue and yellow with clearly delineated markings and edgings of black.

Yellow blends to almost yellowish orange in a band around their neck that looks like a bold necklace.

The females are dull-colored and a non-descriptive, olive drab. Males are gorgeous in brilliant, striking primary colors that seem sleek, even glowing.

Cholorphonia's inhabit the islands in the Lesser Antilles and form small groups, wandering on the edge of small forests foraging for berries using their Finch-like bills to pick up small, tender flowering fruit buds.

Their favorite food is the white mistletoe berry, a symbol of Christmas to Christians.

Mistletoe blooms unfailingly at Christmas and the euphonias are eagerly waiting for this tempting treat.

The tiny euphonia is more often heard than seen, twittering under tree tops, singing and giving a variety of calls, which include sharp, metallic "chi-chink" or a tinkling "Ti-tit-ti-tit-ti-tit," in rapid cadence, calling attention to their happiness and usual on-going busyness. These are cheerful, bright, happy little birds that are much admired.

Chlorophonia's hang around cultivated fields hoping to collect the seeds that fail to get buried in the earth.

Euphonias roam in pairs or like to be in small groups.

They breed in April and readily assemble materials for a nest as a matter of their chosen routine.

Clever little females build round, domed nests in a thick well secured vine or in trees or tall shrubs held in place by large stems and branches on which the cumbersome nest is firmly hooked.

The female meticulously lines the interior of the nest with red leaves to stimulate the growth and activity of her chicks.

She allows the male to assist, but this is mostly the female's primary performance and a matter of routine.

In her carefully constructed domed nest she lays four spotted eggs and then remains alone with the nest and the eggs for approximately two weeks, incubating the eggs.

Once hatched, the birds take up to 22 to 24 days to fledge,(get ready to leave the nest for good.)

This is when the male comes in and helps to feed the chicks. Both parents take turns going to eat and fly back to the nest to regurgitate down the gullets of their chicks who open their beaks wide to receive this much desire sustenance. Later, the parents take turns standing at the entrance to the nest, popping bits of food into their young chick's beaks. Because the nest is covered with a dome, it is very private and insulated and encourages the chicks to stay in the nest longer than usual.

These delightful little birds sing prettily and are heard everyday. They are cheerful and like to express their happiness and purpose in being alive.

BROWN PELICAN

Pelecanus occidentalis

Length: 48 inchess

The Pelecanus species relate to the oldest fossil of any bird in the world, one hundred million years old.

The chief similarity between the six families of large aquatic fish eating birds called Steganopodes swimmers, is their feet. These are the only birds with all four toes webbed. Pelicans have short strong legs and large expansive wings with eleven primary coverts in descending lengths. They look clumsy walking as their bodies are large and cumbersome on land. They have a difficult time balancing considering the large gular pouch that forms the lower part of their large bill.

Pelicans are excellent fliers and swimmers. The water is their home and they love being in it.

Pelicans are graceful for large fliers and strong swimmers even in rough seas.

Mates are chosen for life. Sometimes they flock in groups and are seldom alone for they are gregarious and like to be around the bustle of humanity, the ocean, boats and marinas. They can be found hovering over or hanging around every marina in the islands.

Pelicans fly over the water looking for fish. Spotting fish, they dive at break-neck speed at a 40 degree slant, their wings open until the last moment before striking water. They may dive from as high as 50 feet and hit the water hard and fast.

Underwater their pouch opens wide sifting fish and water through its mandibles. The pouch holds 2 1/2 gallons of fish on one dive alone.

This large bird does not desert the sea except to follow the fish into the lagoons and smaller bodies of water like the cattle ponds where the pelican can feast at will by the usual diving into large schools of fish in shallower water.

Gulls often accompany pelicans for they are avid fishers and assured they wil eat their fill from what is let over by the pelicans from the largess of the enormous gular pouch. Happily the accompanying birds never go hungry. There is enough for all to share and Pelicans are generous.

Underwater the gular pouch extends greatly as the mandibles expand outward forming into a large scoop capable of catching gallons of water in which many fish are trapped, carried out of the water and eaten later.

The big bill rests on the Pelican's foreneck in flight or when the bird is sleeping. This gregarious bird, feeds and roosts with hundreds or thousands of pelicans, gulls and terns. Pelicans are found on beaches, piers or pilings, barges, boats, and in dense vegetative mangroves where plentiful food is avaialbe and the bushes are dense.

Pelicans breed in colonies in mangroves, swamps, marshes, on barrier reefs, islets or islands, anywhere there is water, warmth and plentiful food.

You can identify a pelican by its distinctive flap and glide sound overhead. They beat and then catch updraft currents and soar for long periods in silence. Pelicans make no sounds except when breeding where they grunt & hiss at each other happily.

Pesticides almost wiped out the Pelicans but they have made a happy recovery and are not threatened. Protected chicks finally fledge but it may take months before they can fly well and want to leave the nest and the parent's care.

BURROWING OWL

Speotyto cunicularia

Length: 9 inches

Perhaps the owl appears wise because it says nothing. One reason owls stir fear and mistrust is due to their call which can be chilling, like the sound of weird wailing rather than the sweet cooing and trilling sounds they also make so easily. Males and females sing pleasant duets in varied pitches. If annoyed or mad they clack loudly with their bills, but they can make a dreadul racket.

Their sense of sight and hearing are keen and their eyes are as large as a tall, large man.

Some owls are diurnal, others nocturnal. A third eyelid can be lowered to protect the owls eyes from destructive ultra violet rays.

It is believed that Owls hunt by sound rather than sight. Their ears are large but mostly hidden underneath thick feathers. The ear has flaps of extra skin and differ in size to aid in their hearing.

Some owls have sound deadening filaments at the ends of their flight feathers that bring silent flying, but not all owls have them.

Long, supple necks are hidden by thick layers of feathers. With eyes in the front of their dish like faces their vision is not as good as birds with eyes on the side of their heads, so owls turn their heads often.

Owls eat their prey alive and whole and cough up the bones, fur and feathers that they are not capable of digesting them. They eat insects and also live rodents. Nests are dug in burrows where they lay 1 to 3 white eggs. The male always constructs the nest before the eggs are laid.

CARACARA

Caracara cheriway

Length: 24 inches

The subfamily Polyborinae has 9 caracaras who are prominent in South America but range as far north as Florida, from Lake Ochochobee north to Kissimmee's open, flat grasslands, which are called sandy prairies, an oddity peculiar to Florida.

The Caracara is the national bird of Mexico. This bird is an anomaly, with their distinctive rather long, yellow tarsi (legs) and feet, they must balance carefuly to enable walking on or near the surface of shallow water where they spend a great deal of time foraging for prey.

These are lazy birds and although able to catch their own food, they prefer to take carrion from other birds finding scavenging more to their liking because it is easier. They mingle with vultures and drive them from a carcass for they easily dominate these scavengers by their size, appearance and sincerely mean look that they cast about freely.

Knowing animals are killed on highways, Caracaras patrol roads, lanes and By-ways on the lookout for road-kill.

The Caracara's face is white and they have a distinctive black feathered cap. Their cere and face is red under their eyes and surrounding their curved beak.

Their coloring consists of a cream colored chest, top of their back, throat and breast, which are marked with peppered bars of brownish gray.

Their underparts are white and their long square tail is finely marked with terminals (horizontal) dark brown barring that is striking,

Their jesses (full feathered thighs) are gray / black.

re Scapular wings and greater coverts are also dark and clearly defined, like sculptures. Its tertials and secondary wing feathers are the same dark hue. Its tarsus (legs) are yellow.

Its body, wings and cap are black, in contrast to the white and cream parts, that are marked with brown and black bands.

One year olds are similarly marked and colored as an adult in brown rather than black. Their legs are gray and their facial skin is pink and free of feathers.

In flight the caracara makes a startling appearance of black and white underneath coverts. Its whitish tail is tipped with black, a dramatic color combination that attracts much attention.

The caracaras are almost an embarrassment to the otherwise noble falcons who are brave and hunt like champions, while the caracara seems sluggish and uninterested in hunting or performing any noble act although they are known as raptors.

Its wings are square-tipped unlike the falcon and it neck and head are longer and bigger than the falcon. Like the falcon, its wings over extend its tail.

The caracara can soar on thermals but more often beats its wings and then slips into long glides

They choose a tall cactus or the top of a cabbage palm for their nest, a mammoth affair made of many sticks. Here the female lays 2 or 3 eggs every spring. She incubates them for 32 days. The young stay with the parents who feed them until they are strong enough to leave. The chicks finally fledge but it takes months before they can fly well and want to leave a place where all their needs are met.

CHANNEL-BILLED TOUCAN

Ramphastos vitellinus

Length: 20 inches

With a bill one third the length of its body, the Toucan draws a lot of attention. His bill is shaped like a large canoe and is ornately etched and colorful and amazingly does not seem to get in the Toucan's way. This bright bird is intelligent and can be very kind to its care-takers.

Females are of the same coloring and size.

This specie is found liviing wild only in American forests.

Many are in captivity in very large cages, for they make a decorative statement. It is better to keep two in a cage then have one lonely bird.

If they are removed from the nest and hand-fed they make good but messy pets.

Baby chicks need toys and distraction in captivity. They throw their food around especially when they tire of it.

These are high maintenance birds in captivity because their foods and toys are expensive and exotic.

Toucans eat mostly wild or cultivated fruit and berries. In the wild, their bill enables them to reach high above them with a tongue that is long and thin and extends the length of the bill.

The tongue has fringes on both sides with stiff bristles at the tip. The bill is serrated but the whole bill is very light and weighs almost nothing. It is hollow.

To eat or drink they sip, sucking up the liquid and have to toss their head back to swallow by gravity.

Toucans eat nestlings from other bird's nests.

They also devour all kinds of insects, snakes, lizards and

The toucan is a hopping bird, that seldom walks and is a gregarious bird who enjoys other Toucans, who recognize each other by their bill colors, pattern and size.

With a broken pattern of colors they can effectively hide in flowering rain forests, high in the branches, unseen among the foliage.

They make their nest in the hole of a tree and feel safe high up. Snakes are known to go high in the trees to get to the birds who only think they are safe being that high.

In Trinidad Toucans are never on the ground. The taller the tree the better. They perch for hours. The Channel-billed Toucan is the only Toucan specie in Trinidad.

The underparts, belly, tail and most of the bill are black. The tail, upper and lower coverts are bright red. The bare eye patch and bill are bright blue. The throat is white and the mid-breast orangish yellow. The lower breast has a band of red and another flash of red under its tail as well as patches of orange and bright blue. The main body is a shimmering glossy black. Their eyes are brown and shiny.

Toucans sound like a dog in distress, emiting a high pitched cry that is disturbing. They howl for days and their cries carry for miles, and is not a pleasant thing.

No one knows why they cry so loud and emotionally.

Toucans fence with other using their bills, and pass fruit along from bill to bill in a friendly sharing.

This is not a strong flier and is unmistakable in the air where they are graceful, but weak fliers.

They sleep folded like a ball of feathers with their bill tucked behind and their tail forward hiding their bill.

The Toucan's tree hole beomes quite cramped due to their large bill which is a lot to cope with.

COMMON GROUND DOVE

Columbina passerina (Ortolan)

Length: 6 to 7 inches

The small and very cute, round headed Common Ground Dove's presence is wide spread throughout the Eastern Caribbean. The ground dove mostly runs along the ground with its head down, staring at the ground. Do not be misled, it is only seeking seeds.

This little dove seldom flies but is able to make short rapid flights when frightened into flight and escaping what it thinks is danger.

The dove's call is a long boring coo-coo-coo-coo, or a ooh-ah, ooh-ah, ooh-ah, ooh-ah or it may call out Kooo-pooh, kooo-pooh, which sounds like it is calling out, "no hope, no hope." This however is not its message.

This small unassuming bird has a short square yellow tail streaked with dark brown. Its body is gray/brown with black fringes on its upper and lower back, which lends a sculpted or scaled appearance to this classic dove. The underparts or coverts are white and more white markings show prominently along the edges of the tail. The breast of the adult is tinged with pink, mixed with beige tones etched with dark brown streaks. The bill is almost black and the small feet are red

Its iris is red and the eye ring is blue/gray, giving the small, round eye a gentle but intelligent look.

The ground dove is not adverse to humans who stay in their place and do not bother the bird in its daily routine that the dove views as very serious. Doves accept terrestrial food on the ground from humans but do not accept training from and will not eat out of a person's hand.

Ground doves are found in open lowlands or woods, the dove nests on or close to the ground, near bushes, or trees.

The female makes a nest by gathering materials that she will weave into a kind of matting all with a mixture of sturdy but slim and yet stout twigs to form a base. Then she binds more ground vegetation, grasses, string, leaves and plant leaves, gluing all this together in a messy nest into which she deposits two white eggs.

If she has a partner they take turns incubating, but if she is alone she takes on the sole charge of the nest and its inhabitants. This is a apt, take-charge female.

The ground dove in the right tropical climate and with the appropriate mates, will breed two or even three times a year as a matter of duty.

The ground dove is comfortable living alone or with a chosen mate and is rarely seen in a group or flock, either in flight or on the ground.

The presence of the gentle small ground dove gives a pleasant aura to a neighborhood, for it is known that they flee from noise and danger and seek a peaceful existence. Like some people, this dove is happiest left alone.

They seldom seek the company of other bird species or humans. Perversely they like to be around people, but bot handled by them or need to respond . They want to be left alone most of the time. They enjoy being near cultivated property and are happy with their life style, marching around quickly as if on a mission. They have no great ideas or plans, and eat to assuage hunger and for something meaningful to do. A specie called the Inca Dove is in the process of regrowing a long tail but still possesses the short tail and are therefore often mistaken for this specie.

COMMON TERN

Sterna hirundo

Length: 14 inches

A joy to watch, this perfect flyer deploys graceful skill in the air, with wings beating smoothly or hovering for a heartbeat before plunging into the ocean for prey, spotted from high above.

Often found walking on the shore or on islands, lakes, rivers, beaches, marshes, usually probing the sand or mud for crustaceans and invertebrates.

There are dark wedges among their primaries that look translucent and are tipped with black and have a long blurred dark edge.

Their wing span is 31 inches. It takes 3 years for their plumage to mature and look at its best; rich, colorful and full feathered.

The tern has a white face and light gray foreneck, breast and upper part. Its back is gray. Its smooth well-rounded head bears a shiny black cap. The bill is red, of medium length, slender and tipped with black. Its underparts are a smoky grayish white and its rump is white. The unbroken tail is deeply forked with long streamers marked with black tips. The upper wings are pale gray and there is a distinct black wedge on the outer edge of the primaries.
The legs and feet are red. The feet are webbed like ducks.

Their call is harsh, Kip,kip,kip, Keerah, erh.

Terns fly over the ocean trailing their bills in the salt water. Salt is filtered through their nasal glands.

Terns make a dry vegetation nest on the ground for 2 or 3 olive buff colored eggs spotted with brown.

This specie is endangered and threatened.

CRESTED TINAMOU

Eudromia elegant

Similar in appearance to the ground dove or partridge, the manner in which the Tnamou holds its head gives it an elegant flair of importance that is very attractive.

The Tinamou is a native of Paraguay and northern Argentina, also seen in Chile and in the islands of the Caribbean.

Their plump bodies are covered with tan, yellowish brown and gray feathers that are barred, streaked and mottled. Its lower parts are buff and white and heavily barred with dark and white stripes, making it look highly decorated and interesting.

Their bills are short, down-curving & slender. Their wings and tail feathers are short with the white tips barely visible under the body feathers. The high head-crest ends in an up-sweeping point.

They have two arcing white facial stripes and a blazing golden cere above their bill and between their yellow eyes, surrounded with a black eye ring.

Meant to balance well on the ground, where they spend most of their time, their legs are stout and strong, a grayish blue and their feet have no hind toes; all three toes face forward. Their posture is necessary to keep a comfortably sustained balance.

These terrestrial birds, stay on the earth, but fly with a great swooshing sound to safety on high, where their coloring blends well with the habitat.

Males & females share similar coloring. Females are larger and more the aggressor during breeding.

Tinamous make their flute like trills and pretty sounds

adding to the cacaphony of the forest, safe high in the trees at night.

The Tinamou is non-migratory and has adjusted well to a variety of habitats: dry lowlands thick with shrubs in tropical regions, open grasslands and flat fields, sloping foothills, rain forests and the high altitude shrub lands of Argentina

This bird feeds on seeds, fruit, berries small plants and flower buds, small insects and frogs and picks up gravel to grind its food. It eats certain leaves and is considered a vegetarian.

As careless and unconcerned as they are with their nesting habits, the Tinamou has thrived even though it is hunted for food and sport and yet is not threatened.

It prefers to walk or run away from predators but can rise with a huge flapping burst of wings to fly away to safety from predators.

They are usually alone and seldom in a flock or even in pairs. When they take off to avoid an encounter, there is so much commotion it is difficult for the hunter to follow their flight and shoot accurately so the birds more often escape.

Their 3 to 5 turquoise green eggs are carelessly laid in the open on the ground and have little chance of hatching in the moist forested lowlands it prefers. Amazingly, many eggs do hatch however.

It is the male who incubates the eggs while the female seeks another male to breed with.

She builds another nest and lays her eggs and the second male incubates them for the usual 19 days. Perhaps because there seems to be little partnering or genuine concern from the female, the eggs and nests are treating casually.

CUBAN TODY

Todus multicolor

Pedorrera: carticuba

length: 4 1/4 inches

Todies are closely related to Mot Mots. The Tody family are entirely confined to the islands of the Greater Antilles, with three species in Jamaica, Puerto Rico and Cuba, on the Isle of Pines. Strangely, Todies are the same color as Cuba's flag which is red, white, green, yellow and blue.

Two species of Todies are in Hispaniola (Dominican Republic). There the Tody's habitat is split between the mountains and the lowlands plains.

These are undoubtedly the most remarkably colored birds in the entire Caribbean and a sight to behold in iridescent green, red, yellow, white and black with a black maxilla and a red lower bill that is long and slender, if flattened.

Their eyes are pale gray and their tail is short and shaded darkly with yellow undertail coverts. Their legs are small and their feet tiny with the 3rd and 4th toes attached close to the tarsus.

Todies chase their prey on the ground by hopping. They are great hoppers but on their tiny feet they are clumsy and sidle like parrots, dipping back and forth and walking pigeon toed.

All Todies are similar in color, their throats bright red as well as their rumps and thighs. Five Tody species form a superspecie.

The Todie's peculiarly flattened bills have sharp, serrated edges. Their facial feathers are sharp and bristly. Their eyes look like stuffed animal's eys made of bright beads.

Their crimson throat patch puffs out every time they make their usual plaintiff call.

Todies sit with their heads stretched upwards and back at an angle, in a pose to draw the attention of a mate for breeding. Lazily they swing their head from side to side to catch insects as they fly by.

Todies make short flights not further than 7 feet to investigate prey.

They perch on a branch above the ground where they watch for prey and dart out noisily, flapping their wings excitedly, to snatch the prey, then return to their perch to eat slowly and quietly.

Todies are hunted with butterfly nets. They are friendly if treated kindly and have no fear of humans. Todies take partners but they can clearly live alone and do well on their own. They are insectivores. They live in woods, forests, along rivers and streams. The Tody watches for movement beneath the leaves before darting out to snatch a lizard or insect quicly and accurately.

Todies defend their mutual territory and noisily chase predators away.

To attract a female the male displays, puffing up twice his normal size and makes a whirring sounds with his wings. They build nests in burrows in the earth, digging a tunnel eleven inches using their bills and their tiny toes. The tunnel is long to divert rain and predators. Both parents defend the nest. The female lays 3 or 4 round white, translucent eggs. Both sexes incubate and feed the young.

In Haiti where people are starving, the eggs are eaten. The species is not yet on the endangered or red list.

DUNLIN

Calidris alpina

Length: 8 ½ inches

The Dunlin shares many similarities with the medium size sandpiper with its long black curved bill, short thick neck and long black legs, only it is dumpier, hunched over and plumper.

Dunlins travel in large flocks and fly over or crowd the shore line along the coast in winter having just migrated to a warmer clime. Between the wash of the tide they will probe into the sand and mud searching for prey.

During the breeding phase they take on brighter colors of a rosy hue mixed with gold. Its underparts are white, streaked with markings of gray and black.

In the breeding season they display a large black patch on their belly. The Dunlin's upper part is a grayish brown and their breast and underpart is white with bars that enhance their appearance. There are dark bars along their sides and dark brown or black tail feathers mixed with white feathers. Their coverts remain grayish brown, light and dark even through molting and the brighter breeding season.

Since molting means losing and exchanging feathers, this stage has commenced and is over long before they begin their winter migration, which is often considered a late migration due to the molting season falling so close to their long journey.

Nine sub-species breed in the Artic and then fly to Eastern America before migrating further to a warmer clime.

The call of the Dunlin is harsh and common, Kree, kree kree, repeated continuously.

THE GARTERED TROGAN

Trogan violaceus

Length: 9 1/2 inches

This passerine bird inhabits the moist, tropical forests of Columbia, Bolivia and Venezuela, the Amazon Basin, the Guianas, the island of Trinidad and nearby islands of the Caribbean.

At least twenty species make their habitat in Arizona and Texas. they are also found in all the Caribbean islands before beginning their jaunt by air to Rio de Janiero, Brazil, always sporting their bright, bold, enviable colors and patterns that women envy and other birds desire.

After settling in on a particular island or land mass these particular birds will not move again or migrate for a very long time, unless forced to leave and frightened into it. If however they get restless, they are up and off in a heartbeat, looking for a new, if temporary home.

Trogans will sit very still for long periods of time and consider this part of their hunting skill for although they move only their eyes, they do not miss much and are ready to dart out and catch some unsuspecting morsel. They look for food intensely, without moving any part of their body as if they believe they are invisible and hiding from their prey. Their eyes are mysteriously never still.

Their interesting, short broad bills have bristles on the tip that aids them in catching and keeping insects long enough to secure them with their mandibles and then pop them down their gullet.

This outstanding and most unusual looking bird is called a New World bird, but fossil remains dating back 35 million years prove its antiquity.

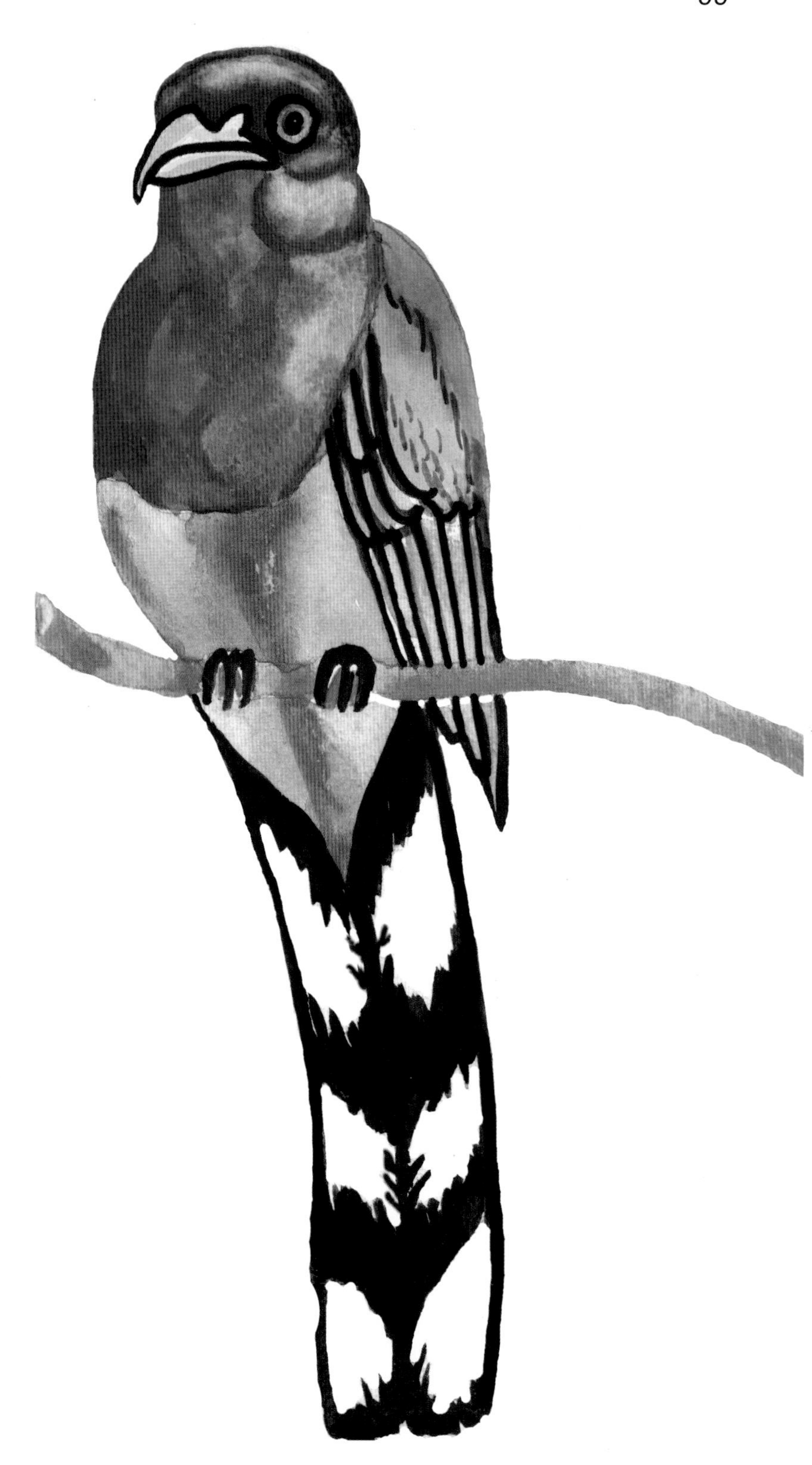

Considered odd by any standard, this bird has two toes in front, joined at the base and two toes in back. Other birds do not have this configuration

The Trogan's wings are also weak, but still they fly to a tree if they see fruit on it. They pick the fruit and return to their perch and sit in silence eating their treasure.

Many varieties of birds over time, lose their ability to fly, and fall victim to predators. Being able to take flight is often life saving. It is not known how long the Gartered Trogan will be able to fly but it may gain stronger wings.

Trogans are New World Birds but clearly they are very old as proven by their ancient history. They are clearly linked through fossil discoveries to the Oligocene period.

The epidermis of the Gartered Trogan is tissue paper thin, which is an anomaly among birds. Their feathers are therefore soft and fluffy and very loosely attached. Thicker or tougher feathers would be disastrous and would probably fall out or injure the bird's skin.

The Trogan wings are short and rounded at the tip. Their tails are on the contrary quite long and square at their ends.

Trogans sing a sad song. Do they know something we do not? Their plaintive call, "coo,coo,coo" is heard in the forest but difficult to locate. The source is the Trogan who likes to and is able to throw its voice to other places while blending into the surrounding foliage.

They nest in a tree cavity and lay 2 to 4 white or pastel eggs. Parents share the duties. More often they will steal a wasp's nest, eat the wasps and larvae and make their own nest out of the wasps's paper-like affair.

GRAY-HEADED QUAIL DOVE

Geotrygon caniceps

(Coquito Banco)

Length: 11 inches

Only the Hispaniola specie has a dramatic white forehead, although there are any number of Dove species in Cuba and Hispaniola.

Quails give a repeated rapidly delivered call: "hup hup hup hup" and end the call in a long slow "Coooooooo," low and soft in pitch.

The quail dove is plump and square looking. Its eyes are red and the lore and eye are surrounded with a black eye ring. It's bill and feet are pinkish.

This grey dove has a shiny purple back, a blue rump and a black tail. Its wings are rufous with orange tips on the primary coverts. It head is purplish grey and there are no distinguishable facial stripes. Its forehead is white from its beak back over its forehead, past its lores and eyes. Its underparts are grey with rufous overtones.

This quail dove is primarily purplish grey with very little brown.

Its food is fruit, berries, seeds, small invertebrates, and insects. They forage on the ground but roost in trees.The dove's habitat in the D. R. is in dense montane forests at high altitudes. They also habitat at sea level. In Cuba the quail-Dove favors dry limestone forests or swamps bordering the forests,

A rare grey quail-dove was seen in Haiti. The D.R. and Haiti have no laws to prevent capturing or killing birds. The quail builds its nest in low undergrowth. Their clutch is 1 or 2 buff colored eggs every spring.

GREATER FLAMINGO

Phoenicopterus reber

Length: 45 to 50 inches

The New World Flamingos of the West Indies have struggled to survive against feathers seekers, killing for sport and for food and of course the feathers.

Habitat: West Indies, South America, Eurasia and Africa. Flamingos resemble ducks and geese except for their physical attributes; and is actually more like a stork or ibis, considering its long legs and neck.

Their bodies seem out of proportion with their necks and legs and yet they are balanced, even graceful objects of beauty and true art.

The Flamingo's three front toes are webbed and in some species the rear toe is elevated but not in all.

These birds, lovely in flight, stretch their necks out straight when flying. Flamingos honk when they fly, (like ducks & geese).

Oddly, Flamingoes share the same body lice with their ancient cousins the water fowls.

In the Tertiary era Flamingoes changed to their present form but their evolvement was slow and took centuries. Fossils of Flamingos date to the Oligocene, some 40 million years ago; as early inhabitants of our planet.

Flamingos prefer to live in brackish or salt water and breed in shallow mud filled alkaline lakes or marshes where they build nests, feed and colonize.

Flamingos have large tongues that purposefully block the passage of food too large to swallow.

Romans savored Flamingo tongues and had whole pies made of Lark's or Flamingo tongues.

The plumage of this bird is so admirable that the birds are slaughtered for their feathers.

European Flamingos colonize and migrate across the Mediterranean to winter in Africa.

Airplanes terrify a breeding colony and cause the birds to desert their nests in panic so eggs go unhatched and the young die unborn.

Lesser and Greater Flamingos congregate in the brackish lakes of eastern Africa, preening, feeding and socializing. Occasionally, frightened by a loud noise they take flight. Large, pink birds on the wing are one of nature's majestic gifts.

A former racetrack in Florida at Hialeah has a Flamingo colony. One or two Flamingos have escaped this refuge, the only one in the U.S., and the birds have been sighted in the Everglades, where these birds are foraging on their own among real and dangerous wild life and apparently surviving.

The Flamingo's nest begins in a tall cone made of mud with a flat top, like a Turkish hat, maybe 18 " high and almost a yard in diameter. The scooped out top is where the female lays her one white egg. Both parents incubate the egg for up to 32 days. Only days after hatching, the young is hopping around in the water. The parents feed the chick until it can fly.

Flamingos feed their young with their top bill, using the bottom bill as a pump through which the mucky goo is filtered. This mix is rich in protozoa, worms, insect larvae, aquatic plants and algae and is the food they will be eating all their lives. They also eat small aquatic animals and various water plants.

GREEN HONEYCREEPER

Chlorophanes spiza

Length: 5 ½ inches

Of the Order: Passeriformes, Family: Thraupidae, a member of the tanager family, this small bird habitats from Mexico to Brazil and is also found on Trinidad.

It is the only listing under this genus who are forest canopy birds, who occasionally venture into clearings, without the cover of trees. Honeycreepers love small fruits and nectar. They also eat many varieties of insects depending on the availability of their standard foods.

These gloriously attired birds are quick moving and attentive to their task as they move through the tallest trees searching with other honeycreepers and tanagers for food.

The Green Honeycreeper has a rather long curved yellow bill that developed over time according to the type of foods that were available through centuries of development, making the necessary changes to survive.

When seeds became more plentiful than flowers, the species developed short stout beaks capable of crushing seeds and nut shells. Where there are species that probe the bark of a tree, bills adapt to a medium length,and are strong, straight and pointed. One of this species has crossed mandibles, a boon for opening and crushing food.

The male wears a shiny black cap that looks beautiful with its greenish blue throat and breast, with green primary coverts of descending lengths that look somewhat sculpted and handsome and its darker green back and green tail. Their head feathers are stiff with pointed tips. Their primaries are pointed and when in flight they make a whirring sound that is easily heard on the ground.

Females are a medium green in color with no black cap and are a medium buff shade in their front under parts. Both male and female have reddish eyes.

The Honeycreeper eats large quantities of fruit and supplements with smaller amounts of nectar, seeds and insects. The young are similar in coloring but paler and do not wear the black cap until they are mature, a time lapse of about three years.

Honeycreepers hang out in the Northern range of Trinidad where birds populate with Tanagers and other species who all enjoy the largely sturdy and massive trees. In these large trees million of birds find homes and move in flocks with a singular intent, to live harmoniously, to hunt and find food easily and to survive and be happy. The Honeycreeper's signal call is a single sharply delivered chip, chip, chip, chip, which sounds more like a Warbler's call than the Warbler.

The Honeycreeper disguises itself and its nest cleverly to avoid predators. It can change the shape and size of its nest for this purpose easily by manipulating and changing the small leaves and the tiny supple bits of roots that comprise the nest; a clever ruse.

Honeycreepers are often captured by hunters and sold to be kept in cages by humans, but these birds do not respond well to existence in captivity. They don't like people either. Many species adapt well and become manageable house pets but not the Honeycreeper.

They build open cup shaped nests in the grass or in a low tree or bush in which they lay 2 to 4 while eggs with brown spots, which they incubate for 13 days. The male helps to feed the young chicks.

IMPERIAL PARROT

Amazona imperialis (Sisserou)

Length: 18 to 20 inches

This is the largest of all the species of Amazon parrots. The Imperial parrot confines itself to the rain forests of Northern Dominica some 2,000 feet above sea level in the montane forests and canopies, searching for seeds, berries and insects.

This gorgeous parrot is also found in the Leeward Islands but not usually on other islands.

This parrot suffers from predators, hurricanes and deforestation. These beautiful parrots are hunted and sold to dealers who sell them for domestication in the pampered but beautiful cages of the rich.

The Imperial parrot is on the brink of extinction. It does not help that they only breed every other year and of the two eggs they lay, only one survives.

This special parrot's distinctive eyes look almost electric as they flare dramatically from yellow to orange/red. (a parrot trait).

Their cere with large nostrils is broad and lightly feathered. There is bare flesh around the rather small eyes. This is in comparison with the size of his head.

His back is green and his short neck is bright, almost irridescent purple. He has a red tail that is tipped with green and purple under his under tail covert and his vent.

His head is large with a large down curving beak that has a pronounced hook at the end of its upper mandible. His tail is short and square and colorful as is the entire bird. This is a magnificent specimen. Parrots talk and sing but don't usually make a lot of sense by memorizing words.

This parrot shrieks, whistles and trumpets for attention and his own amusement. They can be taught to speak and to "parrot" certain words but it soon becomes clear that they might not associate the meaning with the actual word, and endlessly repeat some inane phrase to the point of becoming very annoying.

Parrots are not naturally gregarious with humans. However the human and the bird may bond and love each other, especially if they share a troubled event like a hurricane, sharing danger, they become mutually dependant for company, at a minimum. Sometimes they grow very close.

Parrots feed on fruit, large and small, but never tomatoes. They eat lots of seeds, nuts, flower buds and petals. They love sun flower seeds but require better nutrition than a steady diet of these seeds that rob their bodies of nutrition.

They forage in pairs and small colonies of their own species, happy living freely.

Their conspicuous call sounds like a trumpeting, "eeeeeeeeeee-er," which fades or drops in tone and is not a pretty sound. Parrots are capable of a huge range of sounds and seldom employ the full variety of their capabilities.

Their constant whistling can be jarring. If nothing is made of this, they will eventually stop.

They nest in pairs year round and live in the nest in a hollow tree that they use to lay eggs.

They mate every other year around March when the dry season begins and food is at its optimum.

They will lay one to two eggs. With hope at least one will survive.

Their colony is small to begin with and further endangered so they must be cared for and saved.

JAMAICAN MANGO

Anthracothorax(Doctorbird)

Length: 5 inches

The family of Trochilidae with 330 species is the second largest bird classification in the world and concerns hummingbirds. These unique, tiny beloved birds stem from this genus but finally won their own order.

The Jamaican Mango is endemic to Jamaica and found only there. The Blue and John Crow Mountains National Park attracts many species of birds, making Jamaica a bird paradise where birds are protected by law.

The Rocklands Bird Sanctuary hosts and are care-takers for 200 species that habitat on Jamaica, 25 of which are native to Jamaica.

Principally different from other birds due to the way they fly. Hummingbirds are not only clever aerialists but their ability to hover stationary over a fruit or flower for long sustained flight is not performed or possible for any other bird specie.

Fifty times per second the hummingbird's wing beat in a figure eight stroke like a tiny helicopter. When courting they beat their wings faster.

The long curved bill probes flowers and the twice as long translucent tongue with a fringed forked tip aids in recovering nectar and enables them to sip the nutrients from flowers easily.

The beautiful Jamaican Mango is an exotically colored irridescent hummingbird that has a little twittering voice to express his happiness or summon a friend. They are always interested in other birds of their species.

These New World birds extend their reach far into

Alaska, Nova Scotia and Canada and as far south as Tierra del Fuego, passing by or stopping at the islands between. Yet they have never crossed a major ocean.

Europe has no counterpart to these remarkable, delightful tiny birds, although they are intrigued by them.

This bird is abundant in open, arid lowlands near coastal plains. Jamaican Mangos love the warmth of the sun and seek tropical settings that are warm and moist almost all year round.

They seek Jamaica's mountain range although they do not often live in mountainous regions and they are a bit of a rarity when seen at Jamaica's highest levels.

The call of the Jamaican Mango is a raspy monotonous "chi-chi-chi," a sound like a person clicking their tongue lightly on their palate.

Mangos feed on flower and fruit nectar, bananas, cactus. Mangrove vegetation, nuts and small insects.

The Jamaican Mango builds a nest above eye level in forked branches of high bushes or trees like the Peanut, Cashew or Mangrove.

The males are clothed in shimmering colors as bright as the sun and the female of the specie is a paler version of the male in the same colors although of less magnitude.

Their bills are thin and straight or slightly curved and tubular for sucking nectar.

These birds have many adornments, head crests, chin fans and even whiskers.

Their tails may be square and short or long, rounded or split into two with spades at the end. They can hover, fly straight, twist, turn and go up or down and backwards and are considered masters of flight.

LAUGHING GULL

Larus atricilla (Gulls and Terns)

Length: 13 inches Wingspan: 41 inches

Sub-families, Terns, Skuas, and Skimmers.

A true omnivore, the Gull feeds on animals, plants and fish. The Specie's identification is determined by the bird's structure and coloring. All gulls have webbed feet.

This specie has a long blunt bill, long pointed wings, a short square tail, and legs that are strong and of medium length. This description best suits the Gull's lifestyle.

Its head, flat at the forehead gives the bird an angry look, perhaps as tough as a falcon, but this is a gentle bird.

It takes three years to obtain final plumage. He has a black bill and white head with faint black streaks down the rear of its head. Its black primary coverts have white tips, and a white tail. Its upper body is white as well as its lower body, its throat and breast, are dark gray. Its head is black and so is its back and there are black markings on the wings.

A diurnal feeder, Gulls feed at night during breeding season. They scavenge or forage, finding it easier to feed on dead carcasses or the kill of other bird's that they snatch.

Their flight includes long glides after quick wing beats. They can rise directly from the ocean into strong flight and are strong swimmers.

The gull is common to Trinidad and the small islands off the coast of Tobago.

Gulls are related to terns but are more deliberate and slower than the terns who flit about in smooth well planned moves

The Laughing Gull is related to the Larus gulls that

fly over the ocean picking off fish on the surface. This is a very cosmopolitan bird, comfortable with all types of birds as well as with people.

The laughing Gull eats all forms of aquatic life and varieties of water organisms, including crab, fish and shrimp that it catches by skimming the surface with its lower mandible trailing in the water until a fish touches their bill, then they slam their bill closed, trapping their prey.

The Laughing gull seizes fish on the surface and watches along the surf line for signs of prey or they skim the air to catch insects buzzing around lights at night near the beach.

They are able to change the color of their head cap from Gray to white depending on the season, perhaps using this gimic to attract a mate.

Named for its call, a fast rising "he-he-he-heeee" or "ha-ha-ha-ha," Which makes you laugh to hear it.

When seeking a mate it calls out, "Cheer-ah, Cheer-ah as if to say it is happy and in a good mood.

This may be the only gull seen over the summer months, the others having migrated to the north.

They breed along the Atlantic coast, the Caribbean and South America.

Northern gulls generally migrate south in the winter.

Their nest is a grassy mound on the ground, built by both parents.

If the male has no mate he builds a nest to attract a female who after mating lays 3 to 4 greenish eggs and incubates them for 3 weeks.

Shells are removed from the nest after a chick is hatched.

Nearly annihilated in the 19th Century by hunters of plumes and eggs, they are now safe.

LEAST BITTERN

Ixobrychus exilis

Length: 13 to 17 inches

The world's smallest heron is a member of the distinctive class of wading birds called Ardeids, whose specie is of medium build with a slender body, long neck and long legs.

Its wings are long and rounded at the end. The tail is short and blunt or square. Its long sharp, pointed bill aids in spearing fish. Its head is buff with a black cap and its neck is buff. Its back is brown and its tail black. The underparts are white & buff. There are orange colored streaks on its neck and breast and over the flanks. Its flight feathers are black.

Bitterns are buff, beige and brown with streaks of black and dark brown on its breast and lower wings. There are large golden patches on their wings. They have two white scapular stripes arching over their backs. Their eyes and lores are pale yellow but while courting the lores grow red, to attract a mate. This can be done at will at anytime.

Its legs are pinkish at the top, a dull green in front with a yellow streak down the back. They grow long feather plumes from the head, breast or back. The back, rump and tail are a glossy shimmering black.

These courtship manuevers are amusing and well staged to gain attention and win a mate so their will be progeny.

Its long neck with variegated spinal disc, creates the famous "S" shaped neck while it sleeps but is drawn back into the body in flight and stretched out straight while foraging. During the mating season the bittern intensifies the color and brightness of its lores, bill and legs.

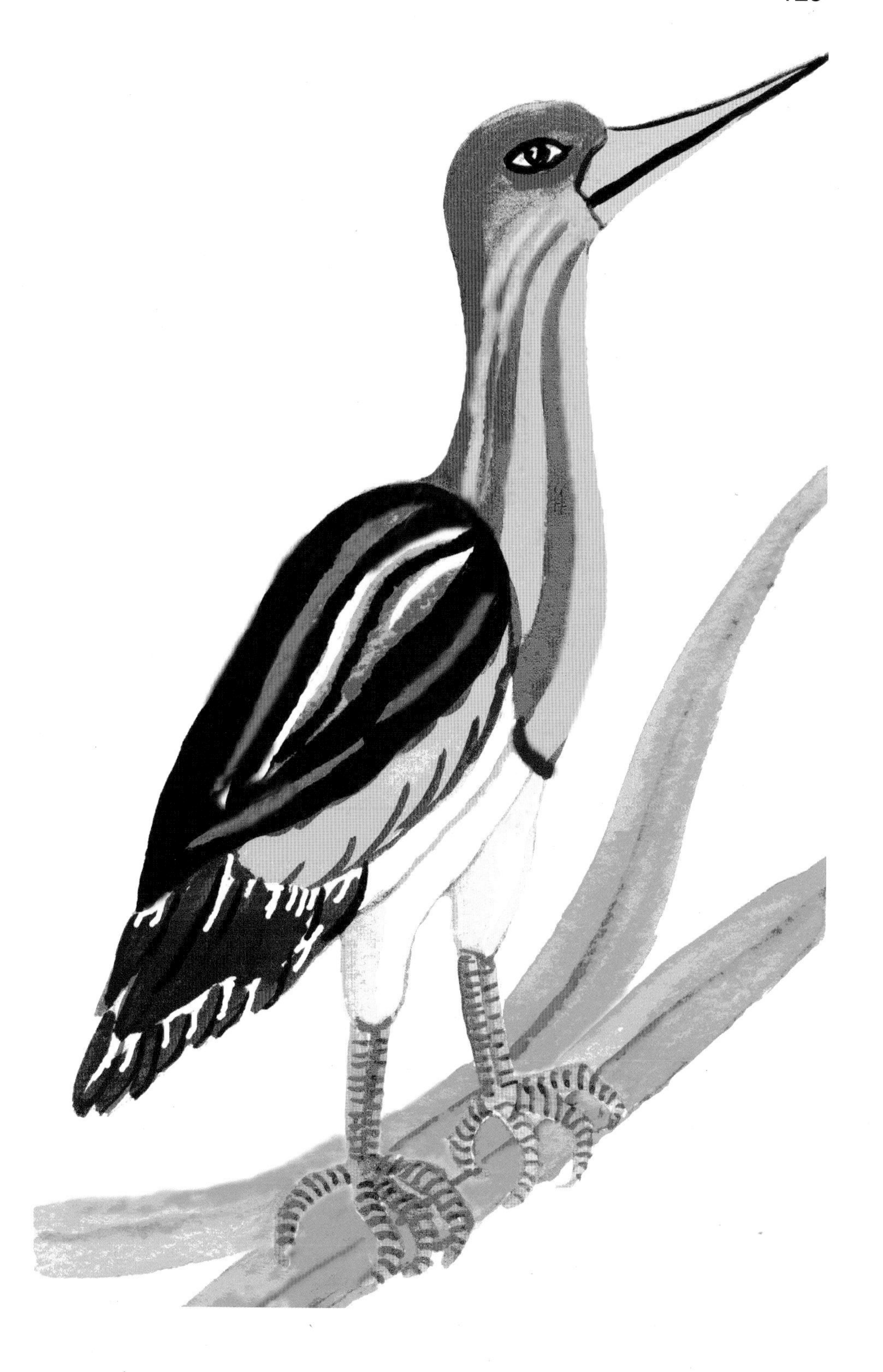

The Least Bittern makes a gruff grunting, low gutteral sound that is throaty with bass notes. A warning call: "quoh-hah.

Their ordinary call: either "kek-kek-kek-kek-kek, or tut-tut-tut-tut-tut. koo-koo-koo-rapidly," sounding like an electric pump. Their contact call is a flat, quacking, similar to a duck.

They fish silently in water deeper than most herons, waiting for prey to drift by, then strike quickly with their spear like bill, using their four sharp, long toes, three in front and one in back to sustain their weight while standing in shifting mud.

They capture fish and small snakes, crustaceans, reptiles and insects, and climb onto tall reeds and ride them to the water to catch their prey silently. They are very aware of their shadow, secretive, furtive and love their privacy.

Large colonies of the Least Bittern are found in tropical wetlands, in the Ever-glades of Florida or on the Gulf coast and in California. After surviving the Old World and the cruelty of the millinery trade three species at least are still endangered and 5 species are found to be vulnerable.

Bitterns breed in dense marshland vegetation. Some migrate during the breeding season in April and stay until August or September.

To hide, they freeze in place looking up at the sky and sway with the foliage. Amazingly, this works!

They nest on a platform in the marshlands with reeds and vegetation. The female lays 4 to 5 pale blue or green eggs.

With a decline in wetlands so declines the Bittern population. One day they will be only a memory unless saved.

LEAST SANDPIPER

Calidris minutillia

Order: Charadriformes, Family and Subfamily: Scolopacinae

Length: 6 inches. Weight: 1.6 ozs. Wingspan: 11″

This small bird is one of 82 species, recognizable by its long, straight, thin bill. Their plain brown and beige colors are as unassuming as the bird itself, the smallest shorebird in the world. Their almost dull colors so like their surroundings make it easy for them to blend with the background for safety's sake; hiding in plain sight.

All sandpipers but one species have a hind toe that is useful in balancing and gripping their food and for fighting if necessary.

All are capable of long arduous migrations from their breeding grounds to opposite ends of the earth.

Most of the family of four sub-families nest on the ground. Sandpipers use abandoned or second hand nests of other small birds and never make their own nests Whether this is just laziness is not known. Sometimes they even use squirrels nests. They nest in evergreens or near swamps in these used makeshift nests; not very alluring or original or prideful.

They dine almost exclusively on seeds, berries and insects, very small crustaceans and amphibians. They forage at the outer edges of mud flats or on the margins that line inland ponds, lakes and small rivulets.

There are many varieties of these "Peeps" that breed here and migrate south along the coastline they follow. Gulls are happiest in colonies where they breed, roost and keep company in mixed flocks. They can stretch their necks out

in flight along the inland waterways, on their long trek by air to southern climes. Their new location will be their winter home in the sun.

They travel in large flocks and fly with rapid steady wing-beats. They are strong, reliable fliers.

Sandpipers can often be seen running up and down beaches, their little, short legs going very fast as they go back and forth over the sand trying to beat the rapid inflow of high tide; feeding everytime the tide goes out. They find tiny aquatic creatures between bits of pebbles and pieces of finely beaten colored glass, and flip them over to discover sea creatures hidden beneath and snatch them immediately.

The sandpiper is dark brown above and a mixture of lighter brown and gray below although they change their coloring in the spring and winter.

They are gray in the fall and winter with a broad black patch on their belly in the spring. They wear a lovely rufous color on their back and wings in the spring.

Their heads are small and round, with short necks and moderately long yellow legs. They have a black rump and a short tail that wags cunningly back and forth as they walk.

Their reddish backs are spotted with bars, spots and dark terminals. They have two distinctive thin white lines that traverse from their top front down their backs. They also have dark vertical bars dotting their white breasts.

Their call sounds like: creep, creep creep, or Cree-et. Cree-et.

They make people feel calm and quiet for these are gentle, composed birds content with their lives and unwilling to make any fuss about anything.

LITTLE BLUE HERON

Hydranass caerules (Pond Shaker)

Length: 22 to 28 inches

Herons consist of 114 species with seven families, and are the largest, most widespread of the herons with five herons in the Hydranass species, with the usual variations and similarities.

The little blue heron nests in colonies in the four U.S. Virgin islands. They are called pond herons and are members of the Old World group, this species has short legs, short necks and moderate long bills. The bill is pointed and slender for spearing fish.

Herons are always near water, either brackish or fresh, preferring damp pastures that incline to light flooding.

They live at sea level in montane swamps or mountain streams.

You may find them clustered at the verge of a rain forest or cultivated land, snatching an occasional seed when the planters are gone,leaving behind many unplanted seeds.

Herons are considered tame and socially inclined, frequenting small villages where people gather, but they also love the open fields and grassy pastures, and colonize in large groups of mixed species of herons and ibises all approximately the same size. They more often make short hops, than long flights except for long migrations.

Their heads are feathered but their lores (around the eye) are bare. Due to back vertebrae of unequal length they are forced to carry their necks in the S shape. This is their assumed position when flying or during leisure.

Herons breed in tundas in the north and are known to

migrate south along the coastline following a long line of Gulls. They are happiest in colonies where they breed, roost and keep company in mixed flocks.

They can stretch their necks out straight but are more often comfortable in the well known S -pattern. For a small bird, its wings are broad and rounded, its tail short and pointed. Its four toes are wide and long, with the three toes facing front being slightly webbed where they join the tarsus. This helps them balance on marshy mud flats or shallow, insecure land

Males and females are similarly colored and closely similar in size and appearance.

Their diet is almost entirely small fish, crustaceans and frogs, insects and small reptiles that they swallow whole. The little blue heron's pattern is to stand motionless in shallow water looking carefully for prey, and silently stalking. If fish come near enough the little blue heron strikes quickly with its adept bill and sharp talons and with the aid of its widely spread toes. They swallow their prey head first.

The Little blue Heron lays up to four eggs in a tree or shrub among swamp vegetation.

The little Blue Heron is a strong flyer. Programmed by a century of abuse, the Heron vacates the area once he hears hunters approaching.

Humans are his enemy. Migration occurs when hunting season begins causing mass flight to safer locales, far from humans and hunters.

Herons take flight when threatened, unlike the Bitterns who try to hide. South America does not believe in protective laws for animals and still allows the slaughter of birds for their plumage.

MALE FRIGATE (Displaying & Otherwise)
Pelicaniformes Fregatidae
3 to 4 pounds, 40″ from tip of bill to tip of tail.

The glorious Frigate is the consummate aerialist and water bird who spends half his time in the air, because his feathers easily become water logged making it difficult for him to take flight again. Therefore he will seek a perch on an exposed buoy where he will fully extend his seven foot pointed wingspan to warm and dry in the sun, before he flies again.

Their tails are long and deeply forked to aid in flying. Its legs and feet are gray and small and only good for hanging onto a perch. Its gray bill is long and ends in an overhanging hook, useful for snaring fish. Possessing extremely light body weight.

Frigates spend most of their time soaring effortlessly and silently in gliding winds gripping air, planing; smoothly and effortlessly, master among the seabirds who fly over land or sea.

His pinkish gray webbed feet propel him easily through the water where he will find his sustenance, usually floating on the surface.

The frigate snatches at quid, baby turtles, frogs and jellyfish all who are on or near the surface. Frigates seem to prefer to be above both water and land and act like they don't enjoy getting soaked. They are known as Pirates, because they steal food from other birds.

On land they are clumsy and require height and a good tail wind to take off in flight.

Once airborne they soar for endless hours, harassing other birds, snatching their regurgitated fish in the air and

popping it down their own throats. Mostly they harrass and worry boobys, seagulls, cormorants and pelicans.

Other birds are not as quick or mean spirited and do not have the mastery of the air that the frigate commands.

Flying fish that jump from the water to escape larger fish who are chasing them, are caught mid-air by frigates.

Frigates like many sea birds, prey on the young of their colony mates and likewise lose some of their own young to cannibal raiders.

Frigates like to live among their detractors to continue their harassment or for amusement. They are highly sociable and like to cause trouble and havoc.

They build nests on the ground but more often in a small tree. The male makes the nest, gets in it and puffs up his gular pouch (under his beak on his breast section), to attract a female for mating.

When he gets very romantic the puffed up breast turn bright red and excites the mate into intimacy.

When the single oval chalky white egg is laid both parents tend the egg and share duties caring for the incubated chick.

The naked blind chick soon grows snowy white down feathers. In three years they will assume the classical black foliage.

Females have similar coloring but are paler and their bodies are larger.

Males are solid purplish black.

Their black feathers are pointed. The male has a band of white across the chest.

Females are marked with a white neck, throat and upper breast that is most attractive.

MARSH HARRIER

Circus cyaneus

Length: 24 inches

A subfamily of the Accipitridae with 17 species, the harrier or marsh hawk is a long legged raptor who resembles an owl.

Their wings are long and thin and end in finely rounded edges.

Because they possess a unique facial disc, the harrier has the ability to ferret out the sounds of rodents invisible and hiding under the grass and weeds.

The Harrier is a ground nestor. The female builds a slightly elevated nest on mounds of grass and weeds. Here she lays 3 to 6 eggs surrounded by tall reeds and prairie like grasses, a fairly safe and somewhat hidden position.

The female does all the work thereafter, both the incubating and feeding. However the male will occasionally feed her. It is an odd relationship. At least he sticks around, watching the scene.

The Harriers are well aware that the rodent population will be after their chicks and survival depends on watchfulness and killing rats before they eat the eggs or the young chicks. Incubation lasts from 4 to 6 weeks. The chicks mature in 6 weeks, and then the male begins to assist with feeding the young.

The harrier courses up and down endlessly, searching and harrying and seems to rock from side to side as he glances from right to left, covering territory and looking for prey. He skims gracefully over open plains and streaks arrogantly like a dominating, self confident landlord.

When Harriers set their wings for a long soar and

are high in the heavens, they look marvelous with their long slim wings and long tails shimmering in the sunlight.

In grasslands and marshes Harriers seek their food: frogs, snakes, lizards, small mammals, amphibians and other smaller birds.

The hawk's downward plight for prey is fast, furious and frantically noisy.

Their tails are long and square, & beautifully marked, with fine, dark horizontal terminal bars.

Their rump is white. The young male's eyes blaze with a tawny deep yellow gray color while the females have dark brown eyes.

Females under-parts are a lighter brown with dramatic streaks and markings and spotted markings on the breast and belly.

This bird harasses other hunting birds, forcing them to drop their prey.

The osprey forced to let go of a fish sees the harrier catch it in the air, flip it and swallow it whole head first.

The Harrier's legs and feet are yellow with very powerful talons, long and sharp.

They catch and kill small birds in the air with their talons. One talon pierces the breast and death is instant.

The young are afraid to cross open water so they migrate following the coastline looking for thermals along high ridges for long gliding soars where they can rest from beating wings furiously for hours.

They fly with and habitat with short eared owls.

With the clearing of more land for building, the population of harriers is threatened and declining.

PALE VENTED PIGEON DOVE

Patagioenas cayennensis

Length: 12 inches

There are 56 species & sub-species in this genus that almost extends worldwide and is increasing in population. The Pale Vented Pigeon is a New World tropical dove that breeds in Mexico, the islands of Tobago and Trinidad, Bolivia and Argentina; all warm sunny climes.

The large, plump bodied pigeon has a soft looking purple head and breast as well as purple upper plumage. Its neck is short and broad with some irridescent coppery gloss on its nape, like an adornment or necklace. Its bill is slender with a soft cere above the bill. Its throat is white. This is a very pretty bird and graceful flyer. It is strikingly colored in shades of purple fading to a cool gray/blue.

Its bill is black as well as the eye ring. The eyes are red. The lower back and tail are drak gray and the lower underparts are a lighter shade of gray. The legs are bright red. Females are smaller and duller in color as are immature birds.

Pigeons are fast and accurate flyers, going in a straight line and using regular wing beats. Occasionally they flick their wings sharply, a characteristic. They are capable of flying very high and very far. They carry messages wrapped around their legs and are known as reliable.

Pigeons feed on berries, small fruit and seeds that grow in abundance in the wilds of the Caribbean tropical islands large and small.

The best places for wild abundant growth and vegetation are in the upper reaches, montanes and foothills of mountains of all heights; places that are private and have

little habitation, especially of the human variety.

Pigeons favor the Hog plum and Guavaberry fruit.

The pigeon's head in comparison to its well rounded body, seems small, this is due to its soft, close feathers This is a smart bird, proven by the ease with which it can be trained to carry messages back and forth or do tricks.

Doves have an unerring sense of direction and always know how to find home. They are small round birds.

Commonly seen on Tobago and in Trinidad in open woodlands and marshes, they are locally called the "Ramier Bird." They inhabit forests and riverbanks and like open areas that are bordered with heavy growth and large trees where they can hide. They are also fond of white sandy forests and tropical lowlands where there are lots of scrub plants and scrawny windswept trees.

They enjoy flying over open plains to land in treetops or high branches as their look-out.

Male pigeons "display" during the breeding season and make noticeably semi-circular flights that end with a long graceful glide to a tree, to attract and impress a mate; their way of showing off.

Their call is a soft "Ku Kuk croo-ooos, a familiar (cukcukaroo).

Pigeons seem content to go through life solo although they congregate to drink together, eat and roost in small colonies.

The Pale Vented Pigeon is closely related to the Plain and the Red-billed Pigeon and somewhat resembles the Scaled Pigeon that has similar display flights but lacks the scaly, sculpted look. They build a painstakingly good nest to lay one egg up in a tree. They are not threatened.

PASSERINI'S TANAGER OR CHERRIE'S TANAGER. Formerly the SCARLET RUMPED TANAGER

Ramphocelus paserinii

Length: 7 inches

Finally reclassified as a separate specie, the family of tanagers is confined almost entirely to the Americas, with 222 species.

Eight of this specie are known as velvet tanagers. They are non-migratory with the exception of 4 species who migrate from North America to South America and the Caribbean.

Most tanagers are less than 8 inches in length and are smart, compact, well rounded birds, capable of making loud, sharp, staccato notes that are easily heard, clear and pleasant. People recognize and stop to listen to them.

Passerini's tanagers have the unique ability to hold notes endlessly and keep singing for a long time, making up for less than attractive or memorable melodies.

Females are alerted when the males start singing persistently and immediately hustle into building cup shaped nests silently for they cannot singat all. This happens before the onset of the rainy season. Females appear in boring, dull colors, gray head, olive upper parts, paler on rump with brown wings and tail. Their under tail coverts and vent are pale olive, but still the males love them.

Males are gorgeous in shiny silk-like velvet in brilliant reds, or yellows combined with a glistening black, as if completely clothed in black and wearing red underpants. Even their bills shine like silver with a decidely blue cast completed by a red iris. Stunning!

These medium size tanagers seem to have no sense of territory and buzz about in pairs or groups of a dozen or so in a flock of mixed birds. They light in trees to search for food and rest before buzzing off again. At night they gather in bushy thickets to sleep.

This tanager tries not to be conspicuous and even seeks shadows where leafy bowers hide his glorious colors. It is easier to detect his song than his presence for they are experts at hiding behind leafy limbs.

In the feather trading days of the 1880, millions of bright colorful carcasses were shipped to Europe, greatly depleting the tanager population along with hundreds of other species for identification and storage as examples.

Rooting around in leaves they find and eat the bugs and insects that make leafy trails in the leaves they have eaten. They also eat leaves but they love berries and fruit that they swallow whole. They drink nectar. Eating is never hurried and food is plentiful. Tanagers troll for insects in the air through open mandibles that snap shut when they get a beak full.

After breeding, the pair may remain together for the following year. They breed semi-annually.

Females build a cup nest on a horizontal branch anywhere from 5 to 50 feet high. She snitches material from other nests, fluff, small twigs, soft leaves, grasses. The male also gathers material. The female incubates alone but the male remains nearby to help feed and rear the chicks. The 3 to 5 eggs are a lovely shade of greenish blue with brown, black, purplish irregular spots. Incubation lasts for two weeks and after hatching the chicks fledge in two more weeks. These are notably good parenting birds.

PEREGRINE FALCON

Falco peregrinus

Length: 18 Inches

There are 35 species in this subfamily. This raptorine has long pointed wings, bare yellow tarsi and feet with razor sharp, long talons. Their thighs are thickly feathered.

Falcons have a helpful tooth in their curved upper bill that is useful for tearing flesh.

This ancient bird was a favorite of nobility and falconers and as a consequence is considered a noble bird. Only royalty were allowed to train or own falcons, beginning with the rank of earl. This doctrine included clergymen in the medieval era. Priests were allowed to hunt with smaller falcons. Ospreys, and falcons are dispersed worldwide.

Once called the Duck Hawk, in ancient times, the falcon was hooded, chained by the ankle and trained to a thick glove. Trainers delighted in the specie for their ease of training and their skill and intelligence. Once trained the falcon is loyal to his falconer forever.

Falcons in North America migrate annually as far south as Argentina to coastal lands and mangroves that are loaded with eatable prey and a desirable climate.

The ubiquitous falcon will eat small ground mammals, lizards and snakes if no more delectable fare is available like a lovely looking fellow bird.

If a Falcon is flying high in the sky, they are easily recognizable by their long pointed wings, slim tails and their large square body mass. They are chunky because they are highly muscled, but still they are graceful in flight and a marvelous looking raptor. Falcons are highly favored birds because they are warrior types and ultra brave.

Falcons call out Kek-kek-kek-kek-kek-kek to announce their return to their mate and the young for whom they bring sustenance.

It is thrilling to watch the peregrine falcon hunt. Its speed, aerial skill and amazing ferocity are legendary The falcon flies several hundred feet high and spotting prey, dives furiously at 175 miles per hour upon its unsuspecting victim, catching it in the air, with one squeeze, breaks its back or pierces its heart with a talon, snuffing out its life.

With large prey, the falcon kills it on the wing, allows the bird to fall to earth and lands to feast on the ground, or holds onto it and descends to earth.

In Japan, trained hawks arrived in 355 A.D., a gift from Korea. The aristocracy loved the sport and put thousands of acres into hunting preserves. In Japan, falcons are decorated in jewels and special colors denoting their hunting ability. Those with purple leg Jesses denote the highest honors. and greatest skill.

A falcon has to kill a large white crane to have his heavily feathered jesses painted purple. Less capable birds settle for red, blue, yellow or brown jesses according to their skill. Only the crane killers wear purple.

Falcons do not build nests but use abandoned nests of other large hawks or crows.

They roost high on cliffs and lay their eggs on boulders. They lay 2 to 4 eggs and the female incubates them for 4 weeks while the male takes turns sitting on the eggs so the female may go in search of food.

In 4 to 6 weeks the chicks fledge. They require feeding until they fly off and become independent.

Falcons have been diminished due to pesticides.

PURPLE GALLINULE

Porphyrula martinica (Rail)

Length: 13 inches

Fossils date this bird to the early tertiary, 70 million years ago. The purple gallinule is a striking looking bird usually a marsh dweller and oddly somewhat resembles the common domesticated chicken or rooster in its habits. It has very long legs and inordinately long, web-less toes that enable it to walk or stand more comfortably amid the mud flats and shallow marshes among water hyacinths and lilies.

Many beautiful settings are home to many delectable morsels of food for the gallinule who is an avid hunter as are most birds who must eat everyday and have to forage on their own for food.

A marsh inhabitant, some gallinules live on ponds and lakes. Others make their habitat in woodlands or even on dry grassy plains, bordering forrests.

Gallinules feed on flower petals, leaves, seeds and roots and they have their favorite plants in the marshes.

They roost in mangroves among the twisted stems of clogged and heavy tree growth or in nearby trees and bushes. Odd, but the Gallinules does not swim.

This Trinidadian bird also hardly ever flies. It is (chicken like) in that it is a slow, ungainly mover in all ways, still beautiful to watch for its coloring and size.

If migrating the gallinule is capable of flying long distances. A few are brave enough to fly over water and are prone to establishing groups on oceanic islands both large and small, where they stop to rest overnight. Gallinules are all over the world although their specie are threatened.

Their strident cry is heard mostly at twilight or when they fly by night.

The Gallinule's bill is conical and marked with a red band over its cere.

This bird's nic-name is the water hen because its utterances ape various fowl sounds: cackling, clucking and squawking. When the gallinule is aroused it makes these odd chicken like noises.

The Gallinule tries to hide from strangers or any type of predator. It appears to be losing its ability to fly over the centuries. Laziness might have contributed to this huge flaw. This bird is shy and easily frightened.

The female makes her nest among tighty covered bushes or tall thick reeds, sometimes on floating vegetation, anchored to the bottom of the marsh.
She uses marsh grasses and reeds to form her nest and lays a clutch of up to seven eggs that she incubates for weeks.

The Gallinule is a tasty game bird. The species has thinned due to the incursion of domestic animals that follow humans wherever they go.

Many of the Rail species became flightless with the dissapearance of their predators. Now this ancient specie may vanish forever due to its inability to keep adapting. Dangers never vanish completely and flight was/is the best defense then and now.

The Gallinules brilliant front shield is so amazing it is staggering to even imagine, much less see. The colors are unbelievably beautiful.

Galinules have added rats and mice to their menu. This helps all the rails who cannot fly away.

RED FOOTED BOOBY

Sula sula

Length: 26 to 30 inches

These marvelous looking birds are most unusual with their red or blue feet brilliantly black tipped wings and huggable looking white feathered body.

Bobbies are tropic or sub-tropic with six species scattered in various locales worldwide.

Boobies for all their size and weight, are remarkable flyers. With sound and steady wingbeats and lots of confidence they spend hours in the sky and are easy to recognize.

Their wings are long and pointed and their tails are blunted and wedge shaped. Their bills are straight and sharp and very useful.

Boobies have a series of air sacs under the skin that help absorb the impact when diving into water from considerable height. These sacs also lend buoyancy in the water.

Their name was meant to imply that this is a dumb bird but this is no longer considered derisive for most agree that these birds are charming and adorable and not dumb at all.

The friendliness of the Booby can bring disaster, as they are not afraid of humans, their worst enemies at times of starvation, for Boobies are good to eat.

Boobies nest on the ground leading to further harrassment especially from domestic pets.

These wonderful birds are found in the U.S.Virgin Islands at Cockroach Cay, Sula Cay and on Culebra and Tobago and they have been spotted on St.Vincent, Redondo and in the Grenadines. The Brown Booby is found on St. Maarten.

The specie is on the verge of endangerment.

Like the young of most species, young Boobys have an urge to migrate. This desire lessens with maturity. When they do escape by air, Boobys follow the water or coastal line to keep their bearings and to be in sight of land for safety's sake. Deadly storms come u quickly and they know tht danger from much experience.

Boobies eat flying fish that are flushed into the air in the wake of large ships. The booby flies across the bow of a ship waiting for fish to surface and then, in a long slanted dive, quickly snatches a fish in the air. They jiggle the fish for a moment and then swallow it smartly head first.

Considered a colonial species, the birds band together to build their sloppy nests of leaves, flattened grasses, moss and ground vegetation.

Boobies do not breed until they are three or four years old. In their crude nest of mud, twigs, kelp and weeds, between March and July, the booby lays one or two chalky white eggs and covers it carefully with a foot on either side, then lowers her body on the clutch for 42 days of incubation. Seldom does more than one fledgling survive.

The partner takes turns sitting on the eggs. The chicks are fed by regurgitating for up to twelve weeks, and until the chick has developed flight feathers. At this point the parents abandon the chick. The chick either remains in the nest or swims away to begin its own life. Chicks lose their baby fat quickly.

Boobies remain alone or in groups of less than a hundred. Loving herring, they dive 50 to 100 feet into schools of herring. Bravely and wisely, Boobies fly further out to sea than gulls right ito large schools of fish. Their cry is a deep squawk, Kak, or deep gultural ga-ga-ga-ga-ga.

RED-LEGGED HONEYCREEPER

Cyanerpes cyanueus azulito

Length: 5 inches

The Honeycreeper is also called the Winged Sugarbird. They were among the earliest inhabitants of the primal arboreal forests that developed in Hawaii about five million years ago. The specie formed and morphed then diversified into many different families bearing great similarities and yet remained widely variant.

Over the centuries their bills changed dramatically in size and shape due to the constant need to adapt according to the availability of certain foods and environmental changes in their habitat, weather, natural disasters, diseases and predators. Of necessity, bills became long and thin to probe the nectar of deep throated flowers. Birds became smarter and began to pierce the flower base from the outside near the stem to sip the nectar more easily.

Seed-eating birds developed short strong seed crushing beaks. A beak that poked into tree bark for insects needed to be straight, sharp and strong so that developed too.

These noisey bird make a deliberately protracted "tsip-tsip-chaa-tsip-tsip-tsip-chaa," in a strange nasal tone. They pronounce Chaa in several different keys to alter their song within their obvious limitations, a common flaw.

The honeycreeper comes in a range of bright irridescent colors, blue and yellow, turquoise and a deep velvety black. They are also red and black or red and yellow.

Their head feathers are stiff and pointed, and their primaries have sharp edges and make odd buzzing sounds in flight, when rubbed together. They seem quite proud of this accomplishment for it is repeated often.

The female is larger than the male. Their legs and feet are red and very slender and rather weak. Our honey-creeper descends from a progenitor who also sipped flower nectar and migrated two thousand miles over open sea to found a new colony on Hawaii where there is a large population to this day.

Present day honeycreepers inhabit woodland copses, loving to be among the blossoming hibiscus and other species of flowering shrubs, vines and trees.

The truth is that they really love more than anything, being in the top of trees on the border of great forests, or even within the forest, and when they have this kind of habitat they seldom venture into the wide skies over grass-lands and open fields

Honeycreepers love the juice from various tropical fruits, bananas, mangoes, oranges, lemon, kiwi, and pawpaw. They also eat insects when fruit is short. They perch while dining, never hover.

With their short, slender curved bills, they can pick up small seeds and insects that they extract from crevices with a bill that was created for this purpose.

The honeycreeper is numerous in Central America, South America, Cuba and the Isle of Pines, as well as the islands of Trinidad and Tobago.

There are many varieties of honeycreepers. Several types are numerous in Jamaica. Their range extends from Mexico to Cuba, Ecuador to southern Brazil and throughout the Caribbean islands.

The male is polygamous and mates with as many fe-males as possible every breeding season. This bird is sybaritically desirous of being among blossoming hibiscus.

RED TAILED HAWK

Buteo jamaicensis

18 to 26 inches long-1 1/2 to 3 1/2 pounds

Called the default raptor due to its command of a wide tange of breeding area, the Red Tailed Hawk is also clever in its adaptation to various and diverse habitats; as content in an urban setting as an agriculture field or in deserts, grasslands, coniferous and deciduous forests as in tropical rainforests.

These medium size birds of prey are called chicken-hawks. There are 14 sub-species that vary widely in color, range and habitat.

Their wingspan may exceed 57 iinches. They are adept, strong, fliers. Females weigh 25%more than males.

Coloringand markings vary from dark to rufous to pale tones. Their build is chunky, full bodied andstrong. Their red tails are short, blunted and square.

These birds are easily trained in their first year and not thereafter. Falconers love them and know them to be great hunters and companions.

Indians consider them sacred and use their feathers in ceremonial symbols and create headdresses resembling them. In flight hawks soar, glide, beat and kite. They eat snakes, rodents,small mammals, other birds and vie with their predators over carrion. Among humans they forage in garbage bins and compete with domestic animals for handout of garbage and food scraps.

Typical of raptors, their bills are hooked. Their cere beak,legs and feet are bright yellow. They incline towards albinism. White hawks are not a rarity. The top of their head is flat and their eyes swift and penetrating.

Red-billed Streamertail

Trochilus polytmus (Hummingbird)

Length: 10 inches

There are 319 species of hummingbirds that are the delight of the western hemisphere,in their brightly decked out coat of many colors that inspire artists and bring people to know and love the creatures of the bird world. Hummingbirds display beauty, charm and whimsical behavior bytheir complete and utter dexterity.

These precious birds are the likely descendants of the Swift, from a long ago Tertiary era some 50 million years past during the Eocene period.

They originated in South America and moved through the centuries southward to Tierra del Fuego and thence to the north as far as Alaska, Quebec and Nova Scotia. However, they have never crossed the Atlantic Ocean so Europe has no bird their equal or nearly comparable.

Hymmingbirds have high energy levels that comes from sipping sustenance from flowers, their main source of nourishment. Nectar has sugar and is a high container of proteins, mainly from the insects that infest the flower's stamen. Few birds live solely on nectar and no other bird can sip nectar while in flight, hovering over theflower with rapidly beating wings, with their tongue that is longer than their bill, protruding down the tubular throat of the flower. On the end of their tongue is a brush that nectar adheres to, making it easier for the bird.

The adult male has two long black tail feathers that cross and are uniquely fluted and scalloped. The bird rubs these tails together in flight creating a high pitched humming that is the signature of this specie.

This bird raids spider's webs and seeks bugs and insects in foliage.

They look lovely in flight. Their tails resemble coat-tails so Jamaicans call them "The Doctor Bird."The Red-billed Streamertail is found only in Jamaica today and is the most widespread and abundant bird there. Its call is heard in long, deliberate sounds,"tee-tee-tee-tee." in zones between the highest mountain ranges to the rain-forests, down to the seni-arid lowlands where they are plentifold if not ubiquitous.

This is the prettiest,most spectacular looking bird in the panoply of the West Indies Hummingbirds, where many birds are outstandingly gorgeous and unique.

Since the Hummingbird's legs and feet are tiny and weak, they fly everywhere, even over short distances that are no more than a hop away.

They are well known because of the noise they make wby rubbing their tails together and their unbelievably beautiful appearance and their overall cunningness with their bright green color topped by a shiny black cap and a bright red long bill that is tipped with black.

The female uses the finely spun threads from the spider's web that she carefully harvests to bind the ingredients of her nest together. She uses down from certain plants and green moss of the softest variety before laying two white eggs the size of beans in her nest.

Alone she incubates her eggs for two to three weeks and then feeds the chicks that are born bald. Amazingly, the chicks are ready to leave the nest in three weeks,at which time they have their feathers although they are not big or yet strong enough to be independent.

REDDISH EGRET

Egretta rufescens

Order: Ciconiformes

Family: Ardeida

Height: 27 to 32"tall, Length: 2 ½ feet,

Weight: 2 pounds, Wingspan: 46" to 49"

This beautiful heron is a long necked wading bird. Its habitats are Central America, the Caribbean, the U.S. Gulf states the southern states and California.

Only 2000 mating pairs are left, mostly in Texas where they breed in semi-tropical swamps. The specie is endangered.

The Reddish Egret is a medium size bird, slender and tall with long legs and a long neck. It has two morphs: a white and a dark phase where the body is a deep gray blue. Its head is thick with plumes of shaggy reddish feather, hanging from its chest. In the white stage it is entirely white.

Its bill is long, and pointed, pink at the cere and black at the tip. Both legs and feet are a deep blue. Both sexes are similar. Young birds are mostly brown until they mature. The variance in their spinal cord causes the neck to be S shaped and they keep this form while flying, standing or sleeping.

Colonies dwindled drastically in the last century when their elegant plumage was desired by hat makers. Now their habitat is being destroyed.

In Texas and Florida these birds live year round on the gulf coast, in Mexico, the Caribbean, Costa Rica, Columbia and Venezuela.

These are 100% salt water birds, living and breeding in coastal tidal flats,brackish lagoons, salt water marshes,

estuaries and mangroves.

They eat fish, frogs and crustaceans, and wade about until they find prey and then start running after it with their wings spread wide comically. They jump, twist and run sideways to catch a fish. They hold their wings wide with the sun behind them, creating a deep shadow on the water to attract and confuse fish.

Some birds migrate further south than Texas, probably as far as South America where they breed and then return to Texas once their chicks are gone.

Natural predators who eat their eggs and young of the egrets are, great tailed grackles, dogs, rats, foxes, cayotes, racoons, falcons, vultures and hawks.

A mating male has a large plumage ruff surrounding his head to attract a mate.

This Egret makes a variety of interesting sounds. Away from the colony it merely grunts and gives out low, soft, self pitying, almost human groans.

They reach sexual maturity at 3 or 4 years and mate between March and July.

Like herons and wading birds, they nest in colonies & build, a nest some 10 inches thick, 25 inches wide on the inside, on the ground or they erect a platform of sticks and reeds, from 3 to 15 feet above water.

The parents build together. The female deposits 3 or 4 light blue/green eggs. Both parents incubate and feed the young.

The chicks fledge in four weeks and fly away at 7 weeks. The parents watch over them and feed them until they are independent. The Egret forms into colonies with other herons, cormorants, spoonbills and Ibises.

ROSEATTE SPOONBILL

Ajaja ajaja

Length: 32 inches

Height: 50 inches

This flamboyant and unusual looking bird is considered a bit strange looking, but wondrous all the same, considering its pink and red feathers and brilliant white plumage, its long curving neck and the oddest broad ,flaring flat, long curving bill that typifies its name and looks like a large handled spoon.

The wings and back are pink and red and their neck and chest is white with a tuff of red feathers. Their heads are rather greenish white with a black band like a collar extending around the back of their head, coming to the front just under the bird's eyes. There are no other feathers on this rather green grayish head.

The upperbill is gray with black markings and stripes seven inches long. Their eyes are red, as are their feet and legs. Their rump is red and their tail is yellowish, orange, pinkish, red and their red and pink wings bear wide red carpal barring.

The young have different body and feathers coloring.

Spoonbills differ from their close cousin, the Flamingo, due to their shorter legs, necks and bills that are more stout. This is the most unusual bill in the wading bird kingdom, and yet it is well suited to their feeding habits.

The Spoonbill is mostly silent but may set up a variety of low guttural grunts, clucking and clacking when desirous of a mate. They make peculiar sounds when eating to show pleasure. They are rarely found inland but are plentifold in inland estuaries and lagoons where they

find abundant insects, worms, crustaceans, fish, amphibians, invertebrates and plants.

They eat by submersing their enormous bills half open under water, trolling back and forth as they move forward, skimming the water looking for live creatures. The bill closes quickly on anything ateable.

The birds are non-migratory but usually disperse after breeding in the states along the U.S. gulf or in South Atlantic coastal lands.

They fly in flocks and are highly sociable and nest in mixed breeds, of ibises, herons, cormorants and spoonbills.

The population decreased during the years when women wore hats and the Spoonbill's gorgeous feather were in high demand. Even royalty bowed to the use of the elegant, brilliantly colored feathers of the Roseatte Spoonbill and especiallyAmericans who flocked to be presented at Court during the nineteenth century as was the fashion.

The flocks are recovering and populating again, but are only protected in the U.S. Most countries do nothing to protect their birds but they are learning and beginning to change this policy due to increased appreciation of birds.

Flocks are still however diinishing along the various coasts where the Roseatte Spoonbills are prone to habitate.

Spoonbills are fast flyers, flying with their long necks extended and with their long legs, stretched out straight. Their pattern is to beat their wings regularly and evenly and then to soar and glide when possible. They fly quite high and catch the thermal winds that help to lift their wings and aid in a pleasant flight.

In large groups they form a V-shaped diagonal line with respect to each bird's integral position.

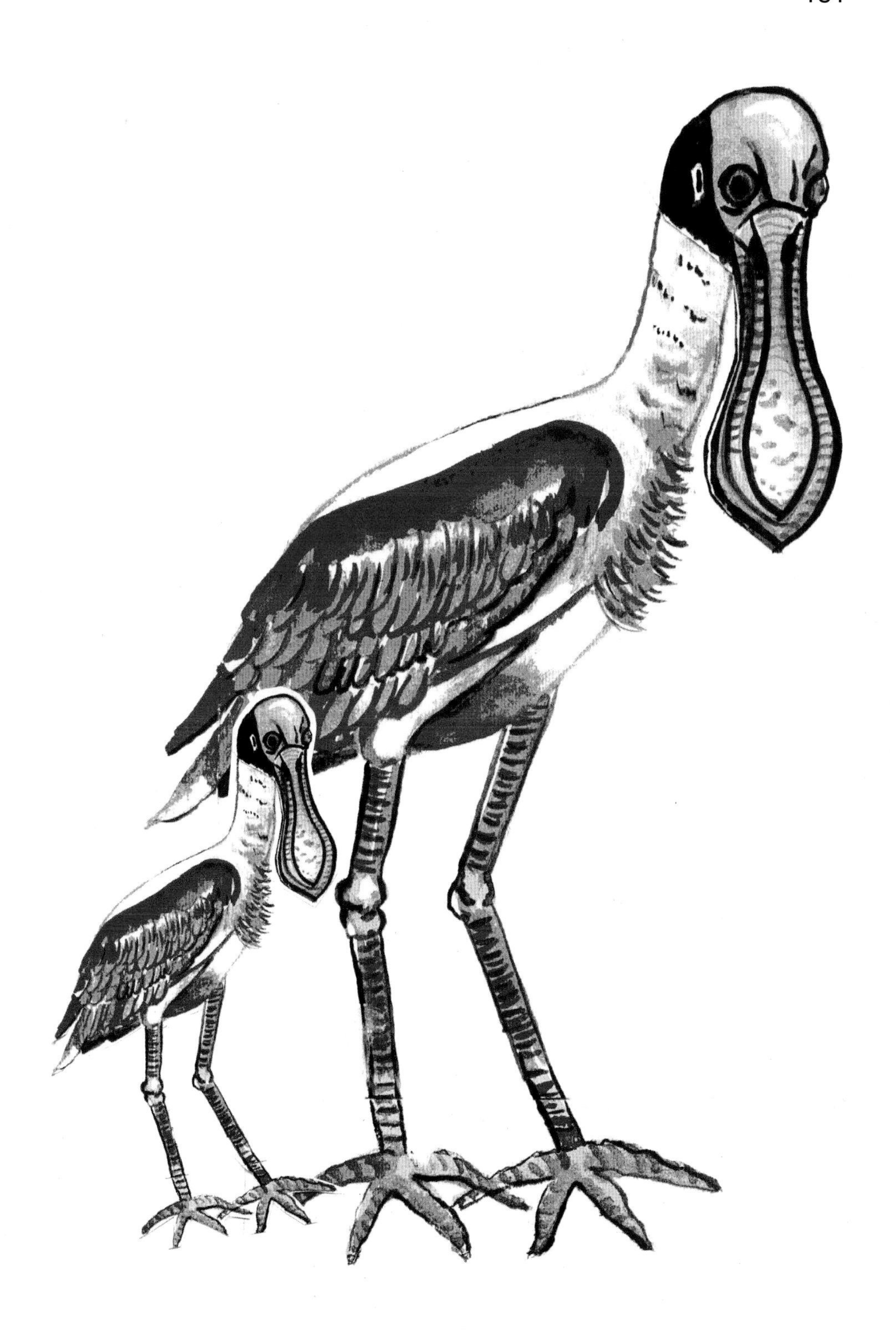

ROYAL TERN

Thalasseus maximus

Length: 20 inches

Terns share similarities with gulls but are more slender and graceful even though they fly with their heads and bills tucked down. They do not soar, but fly with a steady beat of their wings. When hunting, they sight from the air and dive into the water to snatch minnows or shrimp.

Terns catch insects on the wing and take the food they need from the ocean. They rise from the sea with fish in their beak and fly to a solid surface to eat. They are web footed but their feet are too small for their size and therefore inadequate to propel them as a swimming aide. Terns are white bodied with gray backs and dark markings on the covert edges of their wings. They wear a black top cap extending to a bristly crest that protrudes behind their head during the mating season. They have a white eye ring in a black mask and a large, dark patch on their belly during breeding season.

Their tails are long and forked. The Royal Tern has black legs of medium length and girth. Juveniles do not mature or breed until they are three.

Their bills are orange/red, slender but strong, and they open very wide. The Royal Tern is white all over with darker wings and a wingspan of 52 inches. The sexes are similar in color. Both call out repeatedly "Keer-reet, Keer-reet." They are fond of flocking together. Their nest is a crude affair of dry material on the ground, which the parents defecate on to waterproof and to harden the rim.

Hundreds of chicks congregate in a communal creche fed by their individual parents who know their young.

RUFOUS BROWED PEPPERSHRIKE

Cyclarhis gujanensis

Length: 6 1/2 inches

The peppershrike is a passerine bird from the family Vireos, the first of six families that contain one tenth of the world's birds, or 800 species.

This family's distribution is centered in the tropics where all of these true temperate zone breeders from the north migrate to the American tropics for the winter, perhaps their original ancestral home.

The name rufous comes from the rufous line of coloring around the peppershrike's brow line. It other colors are prominently yellow and pale blue and very bright and lovely.

Its head is large and solid looking and its bill is of a serious nature. The gray head has a rufous brow with green upper parts, yellow throat and lowerparts , with yellow fading to white on the belly.

Peppershrikes like to roost on the outer limbs of trees or large bushes where they hop about or run up and down the branches searching for insects, or picking up seeds or berries. Their favorite berries are the elderberry, huckleberry, pokeberry or magnolia. The elderberry when ripe can get them quite drunk and make them pesky to humans and birds.

This noisy persistent singer sings a cadence of several musical notes and may vary them or sing tthe same phrase and notes a hundred times in endless repetition. Its dull prattling monologues led the early settlers to dub this bird "the preacher." It will sing all day through dusk both spring and summer. Its musical phrases employ 3 to 5 notes.

They may create a pleasant melody with lovely tonal qualities restructured at will when they please.

Not a strong flier, the peppershrike when discovered is usually in the forest or lightly wooded areas of Trinidad and seldom fly out in the open over grasslands or flattened fields for fear of predators who are seen snatching birds out of the air.

They inhabit known bush-lands and live on the inner margins of forests, at the edge of clearings in tropical zones, where cultivation by humans takes place.

They are often seen pacing on the ground looking for insects large and small. They hold their prey with their strong feet and rip the flesh apart with their equally strong beaks. They usually land to devour their prey.

They can fly but do so un-inspiringly and weakly and would rather be on the ground or perched on a limb. Given to singing 1000 songs a day. If they are annoyed or angry, they make loud, ugly scolding sounds, leaving no doubt that birds have emotions and intelligence and are both happy, sad and capable of anger.

With his strong powerfully hooked beak, the peppershrike eats many varieties of spiders and large insects, even those with tough hides that he crushes before devouring.

The breeding season commences for the peppershrike when the seasonal rains begin.

A hastily built cup nest is slung between the crook of two branches like a hammock, as high as possible in the cover of leaves and tall trees. Here three pinkish white eggs are laid, all marked with brown irregular spots. Further studies are underway to determine the exact nature and habits of this charming bird who is a bit of a mystery.

SAFFRON FINCH

Sicalis flaveola FAmily: Fringillidae

Length: 6 inches

The Saffron Finch is part of the Sparrow and Finch family with at least 690 species called Seedeaters. They have beaks suitable to collecting seeds, their bills being short, stout and pointed. These beaks are stronger than they appear.

This genus passerine (song birds with perching habits) have been on earth for 30 million years. Passer is Latin for Finch.

These birds habitate are all over the world except in the Ant-Artic. They originated in South America from north to south and are also found in Columbia, Venezuela,, Ecquador, Peru, Brazil, Argentina, Guyana, Jamaica, Suriname and the Netherlands where they habitat in lowland brush, grasslands, and fields under cultivation on the border of the Amazon Basin. This is due to the natural support of abundant plant food that produces eatable seeds and berries to sustain this specie.

This bird is closely allied genetically with Tanagers who have similar anatomical and behavorial similarities,besides shared daily traits. Both ar good singers, foraging on the ground, being strong fliers, gregarious of nature but are not the migrating kind. They both winter in flocks and choose partners every spring for breeding purposes.

The Saffron Finch has a bright yellow body and an orange crown that is tinged with rose. Its back is etched in fine black lines as are the wings coverts and tail feathers.

Its eyes are black with a blackeye ring surrounding the area. The maxilla (upper mandible) is almost black and the lower mandible is buff colored.

The Finch's food consists of wild seeds,worms, small invertebrate's larvae, berries and insects.

Their favorite habitat is lowland brush or open grasslands where semi-culvitated or plain fields are accompanied by occasional human beings planting. They are often found bordering the lands surrounding the Amazon Basin country. Saffron Finches are often captured and forced into cages. They have been known to breed in captivity and are funny and delightful birds who adjust to living in cages although that life has attributed to making them more aggressive than if they were allowed to live free. They do not take kindly to less aggressive birds and want gregarious and equally out-going birds as company.

Most birds grow more aggressive during breeding season and this is definately so with the Saffron Finch. Like all Finches they are hardy and have a very pleasant sounding song which consists of a series of chirping, twittering, trilling and chirping. We leave out whistling for they are either not good at whistles or do not like them. All together their voice is melodious and pleasant, if repetive, hence a bit boring if they fail to vary their tones and inflections as they are perfectly capable of doing so.

The female builds a nest by cramming straw and feathers into a crevice, hole in a tree, or a large crack near a thicket or in scrub bushes. Sometimes they use abandoned nests 4 inches in diameter, that are made of mud.

The female incubates 3 to 5 buff colored eggs with finely etched spots for approximately two weeks. Both parents feed the fledglings who appear at 17 days and wean at 4 week, before they are able to fly. A male parent fights with his male offspring out of jealousy and competition.

SCARLET IBIS

Eudocimus ruber (Spoonbill)

Length: 24 inches

Sixty million year old fossils of this specie have been found indicating their antiquity.

The Ibis has related to humans for five thousand years, particularly in Egypt where they have been an important part of the culture as proven by the hieroglyphic symbols that relate Ibis to the God Thoth, the scribe of the Gods, who kept records of every being on earth, like Ashkashic records that circle of earth. In Egypt, Thoth is depicted wearing the head of an Ibis.

Today living ibises are not in Egypt but in Africa to whence they migrated and chose to remain.

The White Ibis is the counter variant of the Scarlet Ibis, primarily different in color. There are 28 species in this family. These are medium size wading birds, some twenty to forty inches in length with enormous long bills.

Ibis are water loving and inhabit the shore line, tide waters, marshes, woodlands and mangrove swamps, always remaining close to the sea.

Whole colonies breed and nest in forests along the Gulf Coast, the islands and South America, often in brackish coastal swamp-land or on the shores of peaceful inland lakes and ponds.

Their nests are clumsy circular affairs constructed of twigs and branches, 24 inches in diameter. Here they lay 3 to 5 white, blotchy irregularly spotted eggs.

The parents incubate the eggs for 21 days and feed their young crayfish, insects, worms, grasshoppers, snakes, slugs and snails through regurgitation.

As chicks they are white marked with gray and brown. In their second year they take on the beautiful red plumage with dramatically black tipped wings for which they are heartlessly murdered by milliner's agents.

Their meat is desired by the locals but sophisticated diners find their flesh greasy and strong tasting much like some game birds. There are ways to prepare their flesh.

Fifty years ago huge colonies were seen living together peacefully but this is now rare and there are no large colonies left. No wonder, the ibis is a large edible bird, easy to find and shoot and provides an ample meal to those without any other resources.

Both sexes have similar plumage. When mature they are a brilliant red with red legs, a long curved red bill with a black distal.

These birds can be seen foraging along roadways for carrion and in marshy green fields that have flooded with rain or overflowing streams.

They feed on amphibians, insect eggs, insect, small fish and invertebrates, although their favorite food is crab. The Ibis is the most famous bird on Trinidad and their national bird.

A shared characteristic is bare faces spared of feathers. Some species have bare necks too. Ibis' do not have powder-down patches and seldom make sounds other than to croak clumsily or cackle crudely as they have no voice box. They call out Hunk, hunk, hunk when in flight, similar to geese and ducks.

They roost and nest in thick mangroves in shallow water, and search for food in mud flats, swampy lagoons and marshes, using their uniquely long curved bills to

probe under the mud for tiny crabs, other crustaceans and small fish that swim by,

They are quite often attacked and killed for their exquisite feathers so they have learned to migrate to safer climes inVenezula as their numbers begin to drop.

As great as 10,000 have been found colonizing. They are equally friendly with other species and gregarious, traveling and breeding in large groups.

Adults are brilliant in crimson with black wing tips and long dramatically curved bills.

In the Carni swamp or the Oropouche Lagoon, they gather in such large nubers that at sunset they appear in a spectacle of outrageous color. Light playing off their variant hues, mixes with the sun's fading rays to create a special vision of lovliness, seldom equalled in the realm of aviary wonders.

Scarlet Ibis invariably roost for the night in one or other of the above favorite places, usually in groups.

When they Ibis flies, they stretch out their long necks and tuck their long bills close to their bodies, their legs also stretch tightly together, straight and trailing far behind in a sweep of color.

The Ibis uses a steady, repetitive wing beat to remain aloft, intermittent with soaring. The flock performs in unison and is a remarkable sight. These birds are afraid to fly at night, being aware of the dangers they cannot see until they are directly upon them and unable to get free. Perhaps their night vision is poor.

They are non-migratory but will disperse and re-appear in odd places. Their population is declining and endangered and found on the vulnerable red list.

SILVER BEAKED TANAGER

Ramphocelus carbo

Length: 7 inches

Weight: 1 ounce

Tanagers are another distinctive Old World bird, first identified by the Tupi Indians. This is a large family of 222 species confined to the topic and sub-tropic zones of the Americas.

They are a medium size passerine bird, a resident breeder in South America, the most often seen and heard bird in Suriname.

Most of the breeds are now non-migratory, although they used to wander attitudinally on a geography map.

Males have a black velvety back with bright crimson throat and chest. Their upper mandible is black but the enlarged lower mandible is silver. They have round colored puffs on either side of their beak, that they blow up to appear larger.

Males and females are decked in bright gay, bold colors that dim seasonally. Some call these arboreal birds gaudy but they are beautiful and elegant if very red.

They prefer a tree habitat and although they are wildly colorful, their behavior is retiring and they seem not to want to attract attention.

When displaying for a mate, the male holds his head skyward to show off his pretty silver beak and freezes in place like a statue.

This bird is round and compact, with nine primary wings that vary in descending lengths and shape but are all rounded and fairly short and their tails are medium length and rather blunted.

Tanagers eat the pulp and drink the juice of tropical fruits and they catch insects on the wing and feed on butterflies, worms, caterpillars, beetles and spiders. They forage conservatively and move in small groups of 6 to 10, singing preetily together.
They like to sing at dawn to greet the new day.

Their beaks are short and conical and slightly curved on the upper ridge. They have a tooth in the front to facillitate ripping and tearing flesh.

Silver Beaked Tanager habitat in Trinidad. The male is blue/black tinged with red around his head, throat and breast.. making a most dramatic appearance.

His upper bill is black and the lower one is silverish. Their call is easily recognizable as it is a sharp, clear clicking or chipping sound, unlike that of any other bird.

When the sweet singing males start their song, the females get the message and begin building nests.
As they have little sense of territory they build their nests on top of each other almost in a jumble.

The nests are built by the females although the male may help supply the material. Females steal from each other's nests, an insidious trait, difficult to stop.

The female will incubate alone on her nest for two weeks. The chicks may take 20 days to fledge. The male eventually comes in to help.

A bulky cup nest is constructed of leaves and ground vegetation and tucked in thick tall grasses and foliage, maybe on the ground or close to it. It may also be out on a narrow limb with little concealment. The female lays two or three eggs between January and July. The eggs are bright blue and speckled with black and brown.

SNOWY EGRET

Egretta thula (Herons)

Length: 22 to 26 inches

This medium size egret is the living embodiment of the Old World Little Egret. The snowy Egret occurs throughout the world in a wide range of freshwater and brackish ponds, lakes and lagoons.

This prized bird feeds on snakes, lizards, small aquatic vertebrates, fish and a variety of insects.

The lovely Snowy Egret is white all over and slender with a long thin black bill. The lores around its eyes are yellow. This egret develops long, pretty plumes on its slightly flat crown, and fore neck. When ready to breed it develops even longer, more striking frontal plumes.

In juveniles the lores are grayish green and their bills gray before they blacken. The mature bird's long legs are black and its feet may be yellow or black.

The Egret is a graceful, elegant heron type from Trinidad and Tobago, they habitat in swampy marshes and tidewater ponds, near the sea, in shallow water, full of insects, algae and tiny water species, abundant with fish and aquatic plant life

Egrets hunt actively and chase their prey, wading or running through shallow water, darting in pursuit. They build their nests in mangrove swamps that develop in shallow marshes, between land and the tidewater that leads to the ocean. These are effectively water dwelling birds.

During the last century Egret plumage was in demand for ladies hats and fans for presentation at the royal Courts of eighteenth century Europe. At the time of the breeding season the Egret's feathers are elongated into strikingly

gorgeous plumes that hang down its front almost to the ground. These gorgeous feathers are especially desirable for enhancing clothing and hats. Hence the bird was slaughtered unmercifully for its plumage.

The Egret is distinguishable from other heron species by its totally white body, bright yellow lores (area below or around the eye,) long black legs with bright yellow toes. These colors intensify during breeding season to attract a mate. Mating is the most important event in their lives.

Egrets migrate from North America to Trinidad and Tobago, although many make their habitat locally and remain in the Caribbean to breed.

The Egret makes a harsh sound: aah-rarrgh, a loud nasal squawk when threatened territorially or defending themselves or their nests.

They breed in large colonies where they make almost no sound, the males taking as many females as possible during breeding season while the females cope alone with the nest, eggs and the chicks. This is not a good trait and hopefully will change for th better with males sharing responsibility.

Egrets migrate in a haphazard pattern, wandering between Canada and as far south as the Galapago islands, touching down in the Lesser Antilles, Bahama and Bermuda.

Now that it is illegal to kill the Egret for its plumage, the population is recovering from a century of abuse for the sake of *f*gaswomen's vanities.

Because it is so adaptable the Egret has expanded its realm and become indeed ubiquitous throughout North America and the wide range of the Caribbean, breeding on three ocean coasts, the Atlantic, Pacific and Caribbean.

SPECTACLED OWL

Pulsatrix perspicillata

Length: 18 inches

There are 133 species of owls, dating back to the Pleistocene era, over a million years ago, when they were a far larger specie. Their realm today extends throughout the world minus Antarctica, New Zealand and some ocean islands.

The owl is a nocturnal bird, rarely abroad in daylight, but occasionally seen hawking at dawn. Their eyes and ears are super developed. They hunt by sound and do not need to see. Farmers love owls, who may happily exist on a complete diet of rats and mice and clean the barn out.

Unlike the Typical owl, the Barn owl has a distinguishable heart-shaped facial disk with long legs that are heavily feathered down to their feet and cover the tarsus.

Their primaries are longer than their tail.

Like the Goatsucker and heron, owls have a serrated comb on the middle toe of each foot, making it handy for ripping the flesh of their prey.

The female is larger than the male. The eyes of an owl that is two feet tall are as large as a mature human's. Owls mate for life and keep the same nest. Owls communicate tenderly with their mates. Pairs call back and forth to each other in their own special tones like they are singing duets and for them this is a companionable trait.

When angry, owls clack their bills, a sharp sound full of reproach.

The Barn owl is golden brown above and white below. Both areas are handsomely marked with bars, spangles and spots in black, brown and white.

Owls eat small creatures that are easily snared in the air. They eat insects, small, birds, rats, squirrels and domesticated chickens and catch their prey with strong short beaks, and sharp talons that tear it apart.

Owls are heretically linked with Goatsuckers.

Owls are smart and have adapted to a wide range of habitats: barren deserts and from artic tundra to lush flower filled moist, sunlight penetrating rain forests.

America divides owl into two categories, Barn owls and Typical owls.

Humans associate with the Barn owl who nests in abandoned buildings and tree cavities, their eerie cry may sound like a human being in desperate circumstances or peril.

The spectacled owl gives a deep hoot-hooting but is capable of gentle, soft hooting, which is more musical than the shrill screams, snorts and weird chuckles.

The owl prefers forests, plains, open grasslands and mountains with abundant trees and loves highly cultivated areas, perhaps out of his unerring sense of curiosity. In forests they look for the largest, tallest trees with ample girth that contain a large hole or crevasse for their nest.

The owl does not always inhabit the nest but roosts nearby so he can keep an eye on it and not let a predator invade or steal.

Their silent flight is due to their soft fluffy plumage. Their wings beat together silently.

Seen often in Trinidad, the Spectacled owl is dramatically marked, with spots and head stripes and dark rings around its eye that make him appear to wear glasses. Humans find owls appealing. For centuries people have endowed owls with physic powers but this is mere folklore.

SWALLOW TAILED KITE

Elanoides forficatus

24 inches

The kite is an attractive, hook-beaked bird given graceful movements, especially in its airy flight. It is a strong flier with the capability of soaring in bright skies and flies surely with such beauty that it resembles the perenial swallow. It swoops, glides and circles the sky before choosing a place to land or seeing eatable prey, marks the location and distance to his possible dinner and approaches quickly to dive on the offered largesse. Their distinctive split tail aids in their maneuvering in flight, while assuring they are most attractive and indeed distinguishable.

The kites have won the honor of being called the most elegant and graceful of all fliers.

The swallow tailed kite has a mostly white head, neck, chest and underparts.

Their long, well formed wings are dark gray and amply feathered with grayish blue markings, making it extremely handsome. Its flight feathers, lower back and forked tail are lighter in coloring. Underneath the wings, the feathers are white. Its head is slightly small, with bright, shining red eyes with black corneas. Their legs are gray as well as their feet. Their vision is excellent.

This is a one of a kind bird, a member of the sub-family Perninae, a hawk species. The swallow tailed kite is the prettiest, most dainty and delightful small hawk of the entire species.

Swallow tailed Kites are inveterate tree-nesters and can be found tucking their nest in the crook of a branch and

securing it to protect their clutch of eggs and eventually the young chicks.

The nest is a hasty, carelessly assembled mess of twigs and sticks often oddly placed and exposed to weather and other birds of prey as if the new mother birds forgets about the chicks or does not understand the need to watch and protect the young constantly while they are in the nest.

The female lays two eggs, sometimes a third and shares incubation with her mate.

The kite is a private bird seeking rare and inaccessible places for privacy. This habit further leads to its anonymity. Not as much is known about the Kite, but they are under investigation and undoubtedly more will be gleaned and shared among bird lovers.

Kites are in the air a lot, simply flying about, as if for amusement. They land smartly on the ground and walk about nonchantly looking for food. They are known to eat snakes and all varieties of stinging insects that they disarm before swallowing. They also eat small amphibians; lizards and frogs.

Most prey is taken on the wing by swooping overhead and spotting prey, then, at the last second ducking their head and diving to snatch the morsel with their strong curved beak and sharp talons, much like their cousins,the incredible hunters, the Falcons.

On the ground, Kites are effective raptors as well, using their feet as well as their beaks to secure food and fight.

This species migrates as far south as South America in the winter. Their large population is on the decline because their breeding does not keep pace with their high mortality rate. For some reason they are quite careless.

SWALLOW TANAGER

Tersina viridis

Length: 6 ¼ inches

The tanager is a New World bird so named by the Tupi Indians of the Amazon. There are 222 species in the tropics and sub-tropics alone.

Only four species are migratorial. The rest stay put in the best of worlds where they love the moist warmth of the tropical variety, the sea, the mountains and inland rivers and montane foothills, the rain forests and brackish ponds.

This is a bright, colorful specie with both male and female equally bedecked like trophy birds.

The Swallow tail is small and compact. They have nine primary coverts that are short with rounded tips that decrease proportionately on the side of the bird's body.

This bird is a lovely soft blue with greenish overtones that vary all over his crown, breast, wings and tail coverts.

The most outstanding feature is the Masquerade like mask that covers most of his face, arcing over his eyes and covering his throat and extending almost to the back of his head exactly like a costume mask. Naturally the mask is black, in bold contrast to the gorgeous turquoise overall coloring that is so spectacular.

Found in lush water filled locations in Panama and throughout some of the most desirable Caribbean islands, attractive to birds and all sorts of botanical species with much of the island given over naturally to undeveloped zones for nature's ideal habitats. These birds fly South to migrate with some of their own species and will sleep overnight and flock with these and similar type birds that are not of the same species, but a nice wholesome mixture.

There are only 1,000 pairs left in the United States. At least this number has been stable for some years. The species flys north for summer and returns to breed in the tropics, just like the human population, picking the best of two worlds according to the prime climate in both.

The Swallow Tanager flocks in small groups to fly over open grasslands in the lowlands, perhaps to land and feed there before heading to the upland foothills to find a mate, breed and then build a nest; virtually their entire life cycle and the high points of their lives.

The tanager's bill is wide and down curving, with sharp edges and a distinct hook at the pointed tip to aid in the food gathering process.

Oddly this Swallow Tanager has a throat pouch that they stuff with fruit that then bulges in a weird configuration. Because tanagers are incredible eaters they can eat the equivalent of 2/3 of their weight every day.

These birds are fast and catch insects on the wing in their clever beaks because their head is very quick and darting.

They may call out unattractively with a squack that is unmusical and lacks meaning except to them. They never sing, but singing is best appreciated by humans or certain other blessed species and not neccesarily to all birds.

Unique to all tanagers, this specie builds its nest in a cavity in the hole of a tree, under an eave, or in a deep crevasse. Some species dig tunnels in muddy river banks to lay their eggs. They are adept at using what is available that they do not have to labor arduousy to build.

The female builds the nest, lays 3 glossy white eggs and incubates them alone for up to 17 days. They hatch on successive days according to the order in which they were laid.

VERIABLE SEEDEATER

Sporophila aurita

Length: 4 ½ inches

The genus Sporophila has 30 species. This New world Passiformes, the third sub-family of Frangillines includes the Veriable Seedeater an entirely black and white bird of small size.

The species has 266 types and 75 genera. An ancient line, these seedeaters have been on this planet from ten to 20 million years. They are found in the American tropics and subtropics, and the islands that lie between America, South America, and the coast of Mexico.

Its cousins spend summers far north along the polar sea but migrate from there in the winter.

Fringilline finches rarely are colorful at all and more often are arrayed in shades of brown and gray. The combination of black and white is a most striking arrangement. Occasionally they are marked with yellow spots, but one has to look closely to notice.

The male is more outstanding in appearance than the plain brown female, although they are supposed to be similar in size and coloring.

The name Veriable refers to the inconstant coloring and markings of the male, who may be brown and white as well as black and white.

Seedeaters, they inhabit grasslands and open woodlands among a heavy growth of tangled vegetation and scrub brush, medium trees and many bushes. They nest in bushes or maybe a low tree but they are not arboreal and usually nest on the ground where they do most of their foraging to obtain seeds

VIOLACEOUS EUPHONIA

Euphonia violacea

(Mistletoe bird, Christmas bird)

Length: 4 inches

This small tanager is frequently called "Semp" and lives and breeds in Trinidad. It is a true small passerine of the finch family, once the most caged bird of all, plentiful and inexpensive to buy and maintain.

This is a talented bird musically, giving way to rich and varied songs daily. The rich sounds he makes are often a mimicry of sweet singing birds of other species. He successfully mixes musical notes with squeaks and chattering along with mimicry for an effective and pleasant performance that is a bit different every time and warrants our attention.

The Violacious Euphonia is easily domesticated and cohabits with humans if not in forests, in adjoining fields under cultivation. It is attracted to second growth forests, cocoa plantations and citrus orchards and seeks the highest branches in tall trees.

This bird likes thickets and abundant brush as well as tall trees in moderately developed forests.

The male is more colorful than the female, with colors that border on a reddish orange shade on his breast that are intense. His upper parts are a glossy blue/black. He has a golden/orange forehead and the same color on his under coverts

Young birds and females are the ordinary olive drab green above with a yellowish green underparts

Euphonias roam along the edge of forests alone or in pairs hunting food. The Violaceous Euphonia's belly and-

vent are the same color on his under coverts

Young birds and females are the ordinary olive drab green above with a yellowish green underparts

Euphonias roam along the edge of forests alone or in pairs hunting food. The Violaceous Euphonia's primary food is small fruit and wild berries. They seldom hunt in groups. They love white mistletoe berries and all types of epiphytes, an almost symbiotic growth on the under and topside of leaves, on bushes and plants. From these they receive the moisture so necessary to life.

The "semp" creates a sturdy ball like nest of dry leaves, long roots and moss with an entrance on the oblique side. This nest may be on or near the ground, mired in mud that holds it fast and sustains it, on a muddy bank, tree stump or tree cavity. The nest is preyed upon because of its availability. Creatures stumble on it. Consequently, it is surprising that many newborn members of this specie survive.

This member of the large tanager family lays three or four white eggs spotted with red. The female incubates them alone but the male helps her feed the young and stays until the chicks become fledglings. The parents regurgitate food into the gullets of the chicks or pop berries one at a time into the waiting open beaks which are bright red inside. Red is believed to stimulate the parents into feeding the birds.

The fledgling period lasted up to 24 days. Therefore it is good that the male assists. It's nic-name is "The Christmas Bird."This bird is in high demand and brings a healthy price. Fortunately for the birds, they are hard to find and harder to catch. They hide to avoid capture and are successful at this ruse. They are not good as caged birds.

WATTLED JACANA

Jacana Jacana

Length: 10 inches

A thin, light weight, tall bird with long legs and long toes and a long neck. This is a true wading bird who almost lives in water.

Seven species uniquely share qualities: exceedingly long toes and toenails that allow them to walk on mud flats using flowers as stepping stones.

Their flight is like the gallinule, with the body extended in a straight line from head to feet, a streak across the sun, a flash of brilliant color.

Jacanas have brilliant, frontal shields like coots and rails and sharp horny spurs on the bend of their wings that are formidable weapons.

This bird comes from the island of Trinidad in the east Caribbean. They are called a Lily Trotter, Spur- wing, or Lotus-bird due to their odd habits in the water.

The Jacana is a fresh water dweller, attracted to fresh ponds or spring fed inland marshes that are favored with fresh rain water.

They love marshes covered with floating lilies and water hyacinths, surrounded by thick tall reed beds of low water vegetation where the wattled jacana lays its eggs on the broad leaves of a floating lily. They walk daintily through the marshes searching for delicate and tempting morsels like mollusks or unaware minnows.

In flight we see an under wing of pale yellow with the long legs stretched out in flight and the enormous long yellow toes taut and rudder-like, stretched straight and tightly against the wind, like part of their piloting guidance

system. All the while the Jacana keeps his neck straight and his head erect, thinking and planning his flight, therefore the pilot of this in flight air bird, looking much like an apparition, perhaps an outer-space alien bird,so large and long limbed and uniquely colored.

Unfortunately the Jacana has a most strident voice, even described as raucous screaming; the worst sound made by beast fowl. The Jacana seems totally unaware that his call is offensive. The good fortune is that they use their voices seldom, unless they are frightened and calling out to frighten their attacker or sumon help.
Most of the time the Jacana is content to make unoffensive grunts or whistles. This noise is harmless and usually bothers no one. Neither do they garner attention,one purpose in using the shrill screaming cry.

The Jacana threatens their detractors with their wings uplifted wide as they move forward in a scolding manner, looking fierce and on the offense. Now they make their worse clatter and waste no time chuckling or whistling.

The Jacana feeds on aquatic insects, amphibians plant roots seeds of water plants and their roots, small fish and some flower buds and their petals.

In the messy, loose nest of floating vegetation that skims over the water on vagrant winds, the female lays her clutch of four glossy, gorgeously etched brown eggs with thin black lines in intricate designs.

The male cares for and incubates the eggs for 24 days and then feeds and tends the hatchlings. He is the finest father in the bird kingdom. After breeding Jacanas form into small flocks and fly in unison over waterways for sport or in serious immigration for the mating is over.

WESTERN SPINDALIS

Spindalis zena

Length: 6.8 inches

Formerly named the Stripe-headed Tanager, this bird is now in a new category with a new name and designation of species. Like many birds it is difficult to trace their linnear heritage as they evolve and morph.

New species are formed after milleniums of time and many changes.

It has been discovered that there are four species in this genus.

This highly decorative bird hails from the Bahamas and visits the West Indies and the Florida Keys, annually. Sometimes they choose an island for quite respite and make it their home for a while and even lay their eggs there, the interpretation of making this home permanent.

Over the centuries their bills have adapted to serve them for the accumulation of food to sustain life, and are relatively short, stout and gray like most tanagers.

The Western Spindalis all have white edging to their wing coverts. Their rumps are a tawny rufous, brownish red.

To add to their dramatic coloring effect, the male has striking black and white stripes descending in an arc from his bill to his eye to the nape of the neck.

His eye is golden colored, ringed with black.

His wings are black but his greater coverts are entirely white in striking contrast.

Most of the lesser and median coverts are white edged in black and it is the same with the flight feathers that are so beautifully marked with black and white as to make this a fabulous looking specimen.

The underparts of the Western Spindalis are tawny, almost rufous. His flanks are grayish and his lower belly and vent under the tail are invariably white.

The back of the Western Spindalis is black (green in some species) with a tawny rufous rump. The long tail is white with the outer feathers lined with black. etched in a striking manner.

The preferred habitat of this bird is to be in any kind of forest where sunlight streams in through the tall trees giving a spectacled almost magical effect. The trees may be tall and majestic and heavily leafed or deciduous. The birds like the feeling of being protected and like the marvelous smell of the forest. They are often spotted at the edge of a great forest where there are low lying but thick shrubs and bushes. They are looking at the world outside their domain.

This bird acts lazy. It literally sits in a tree full of fruit, eating slowly as if taking it for granted that there would always be plentiful food. Although thought to be of the same species as the Warbler this was debunked when it was discovered how clearly mistaken they were about the resemblance for when the Spindalis begans his routine, which is widely variant from the black throated blue warbler it became obvious there was a mistake, for the warbler is an active bird while the Spindalis is lazy and sluggish.

The Western Spindalis's call is a high, thin Tsee, tsee, tsee, which it cries as one slow sylable, or he may sing this in a series of short bursts that sound quite different by combining these sounds "Zee-tit-zee," or this sound: "tittit-zee, tittit-zee." He sings out at least once a day and sometimes does nothing but sit and sing for long periods of time.

WHITE-BEARDED MANAKIN

Manacus manacus

Length: 4 inches

This colorful, bright-eyed small bird is the delight of American tropical forests. This round little bird is constantly on the move and sings prettily to amuse itself.

Their tails and wings are short and their little legs and feet tiny. Their middle toe is joined to the one next to it. The bill is stubby, broad and pointed.

Both sexes have slender orange legs and feet. Males have a black cap and a black lower body and are otherwise white. Females and young males are olive green and blend into the background.

The White-Bearded Manakin feeds mostly on wild berries and insects that they pick from bushes. If their food is too large, they pound it with their beaks until it is soft enough to eat.

The males are vain and show off to each other while practicing for mating. They get all worked up and hop about performing their courting routine in an area they have cleared to show off. They will practice incessantly.

Manakins live on Tobago and Trinidad in deep forests, or in the mountainous ranges to the north. They are known to frequent cultivated regions where there is minimal protection hiding in the underbrush. Mankins dare to show friendliness to humans with whom they come in contact.

Their call is a cheerful, pretty and musical Chirrup, chirrup, but they also can make a loud whirring sound by beating their flight feathers rapidly. This makes other birds look, so it is successful in getting attention. They can make a noise like a firecracker exploding, hence the natives have

nic-named them "the Casse Noisette," that sound like the noise makers used on New Year's Eve, for a joyful display.

Manakins find minimal protection from humans and animals in the underbrush so thy avoid being seen whn possible and rmaiin very quiet iin the forest and bushes. The Manakin likes attention and seeks it from humans unaware of the dangers involved. The natives love them.

Manakins move easily in small bands or elect to remain alone, singing melodies and brightening every territory they visit with their charm and appearance. Females sense the mating season and look and listen for the males to start beating drums to say they are ready. Males are polygamous. Fortunately, the females do not expect more from them.

The male's courting ritual is dramatic and involves fancy dancing and antics, flashing bright colors and making loud, strange noises while hopping around like a mad little creature building anticipation and excitement in the female.

The display area is a clearing between two saplings a few feet apart carefully cleaned and prepared for the performance. The male's behavior gets frantic when a female appears. She watches until she decides to mate. They copulate and she flies away to carry on alone.

The male keeps attracting more females for copulation. After each performance the female leaves to build her own nest, lays and incubates her eggs and prepares to rear the young alone. Her frail little basket nest is composed of loosely woven reeds, grasses and fibers that she hooks in the crook of a low tree.

She incubates two spotted eggs for 21 days, then feeds her chicks by regurgitation. The young resemble the adult female with bland coloring. Males do not help at all.

WHITE CRESTED GUAN

Penelope pileata

Length: 35 inches

This bird is a species in a member of an ancient group of the Cracidae family; the chachalacas, guans and currassows. It breeds in altitudes as high as 1850 m. Named by man eating Carib Indians centuries ago, and found now in Texas, south to Argentina, the Guan is also found on the banks of the Amazon and in the Amazon basin in Brazil, a famous place for a huge variety of birds.

Fossil remains have been found in Florida and South Dakota dating back to the Miocene period twenty million years ago, and to the Oligocene period thirty million years past. These have not been complete.

This bird can grow to 40 inches in length but their feet and legs remain puny in comparison to the girth of their solid body mass. This is a large bird looking a bit like a turkey. Its head is small, its legs are long and strong and its tail is both long and broad. The colors are mainly dark brown but there is white spotting on the neck and breast,with rufous belly and rear parts. The healthy crest is bushy and extends a way down the back from the crown.. Its dewlap is also bare and a bright red. The sexes are similar.

At dawn the Guan is likely to greet the world with a loud, raucous keeleerrrrr followed by quonking and whistling.

Called arboreal because of the amount of time spent in trees, hiding, roosting, nesting and sleeping, the Guan prefers dense lowland forests as their habitat. Because trees ar being cut down rapidly the birds are exeriencing great vulunerability and possible extinction.

At dawn the Guan is wide awake and begins to be noisy right away. He always makes his calls in the morning with the usual quonking and high pierced whistling.

These ground eaters feed on fruit, insects, vegetation of all sorts and worms.

Their legs and feet are small for their size and therefore weak. They have a rear toe that is part of their foot, meaning on the same level as their three front toes; unusual for any bird.

The female builds a neat nest of small twigs and lines it with soft leaves. She secures the nest in a tree and proceeds to lay 2 to 3 oddly shaped eggs in the spring. The surface of the eggs is rough and they are a dull grayish white. She will incubate the eggs alone. Guans form large flocks outside the breeding season.

This bird has a typical flight pattern of flapping frantically and loudly and then gliding as long as possible before beginning the cycle of flap and glide again. Many large birds sound and look the same in flight. The Guan is no exception.

Guans are extremely friendly with other Guans and are rarely seen alone for long. They partner quickly and remain together for long periods of time and may even join a family group of up to twelve members.

The Guan balances itself well on large branches high above the ground and appears confident and even graceful. This is an odd looking but nice bird.

The Guan population is on the decline due to the rapid deforestation and its limited habitats.

The Guan is also hunted as sport and for game food. It's existence is "Near Threatened."

WHITE IBIS

Eudocimus albus
Order: Ciconiiformes
Family: Threskiornithidae
Length: 22 inches Wingspan: 38 inches
Weight: 15 to 53 ounces

Believed to be a very ancient bird, the Ibis was sacred and venerated in ancient Egypt. Undoubtedly its beauty and unusual appearance brought much attention and eventually veneration.

There are 33 species in this group that are found worldwide, where it is temperate or tropical. There is no sexual dimorphism although the male is slightly larger than the female.

Their habitat is in lowlands, along coastal plains, moist forests and marshy wetlands where land is lightly flooded. These birds are waders with white body plumage and black tips on their outer primaries. Their facial skin is red and featherless.

Ibises make a low grunting noise when eating and involved in interchange within a noisy and social colony of similar birds. In flight and while courting, the White Ibis honks. "hunk, hunk, hunk."

These are medium size wading birds with long red legs and slender long down-curved bills. Their necks are long and S shaped due to irregular spinal discs, although in flight they hold their necks straight and appear aligned.

Historically the White Ibis is the most abundant wading bird. The ibis feeds by feeling with its bill under water, probing the mud around plants and rocks for slow moving bottom dwellers. They can spear, catch or suck up prey

through their thin bill, which was created for just such an achievement. This bird is not impressed with himself.

The white Ibis eats small invertebrates (spineless critters, weak and feeble), the eggs of water insects, larvae, grasshoppers, fiddler crabs, beetles, crayfish, worms and fish, frogs and all crustaceans. They quickly swallow their prey whole. Predators steal their catch or their young to eat them. This the Ibis does in exchange to other species.

Several species have been found eating rice and plant food due to a shortage in their regular fare.

The ibis forms into flocks, where they are seen socializing noisily. When flying together they form into the traditional V shape, in a compact, undulating group. In flight, they alternate flapping and gliding with regular strokes. Smaller wading birds follow the Ibises, and dine in their wake on what is left behind.

The American White Ibis' face and expanded throat pouch turns bright red during courtship.

Juveniles have brown backs and an abundance of feathers and only grow white feathers when they are mature.

By twilight the returning Ibises form a huge flock of thousands. Ibises are diurnal, eating, roosting, flying and wading in the day. At night they sleep near their food supply. They move on as the food wanes. Some favorite sites last for years, especially those near the sea. They share these roosts with cormorants, storks and herons, (wading birds).

Their clutch is 2 to 7 blue-white eggs with dark spotting. Incubation is from 20 to 29 days and the fledgling nesting period from 35 to 55 days.

Seven genuses of this specie are listed as endangered or at least vulnerable.

YELLOW FACED GRASSQUIT

Specie:Tiaris olivaceus,Order: Passeriformes,
Family: Emberizidae
Length: 3.9 to 4.2 inches

The Yellow-faced Grassquit is another passerine bird.(Altricial hatched and helpless bird). A singing bird that perches everywhere.

Geographically, its range is from east Mexico through the gulf coast to Panama, Cuba, Jamaica, Cayman Islands, Puerto Rico to the Greater Antilles of the Caribbean. It is also found in Guatemala, Belize, El Salvador and Honduras, Columbia South America and Veneuela, obviously attracted to tropical and sub-tropical temperatures and moist zones.

The yellow-faced Grassquit's habitat is in thickets, bushy scrubs, and wide open grassy fields, lowlands and foothills and montane (moist, cool, upland slopes) ranging as high as 7,000 feet where the weather is vastly different from the low land haunts and nights are actually quite cold.

This bird is a notable grass seedeater but it also eats berries, insects and small fruit.

The Grassquit scratches the ground, looking oddly like a chicken, to get stray seeds or uses its sharp, pointed bill pecking the ground for seeds and small insects.

This tiny bird has dull olive upperparts, marked with brighter green and white with paler underparts with some dark lines and tips on feather coverts descending to a pointed rufous vent.

The back of its head is buff with a few rufous stripes. The back is olive green, darker than its front parts. Its face is mostly yellow with black markings that extend down and

around its lores and a yellow eyebrow with a black cere connecting to a black stripe running down its ample yellow neck.

Its superol is reddish, surrounded by a black eye ring. The bill is sharper than other seed eaters and conical in shape and light grey in color.

Females and juveniles are similar in coloring and size but juveniles are paler. Before the end of the first year the juvenile will have full adult plumage.

The grassquit sings a song that is weak and sounds more like buzzing with (t's) and (s's) that are hissed with a heavy lisp.

The grassquit is similar in its habits,with the tanager who eats the same foods. they may choose to flock together for short periods and may even roost side by side for safety's sake more than anything.

Flight is usually of short duration as this bird is a weak flyer who will beat his wings rapidly ten times and then exhausted tuck back his wings close to his body and hope to coast with good fortune. He will repeat this pattern timelessly until he gains his goal, but he will be very tired and not happy to take to the air any time soon.

The male sings a courting song in slow, subtle tones close up, right in the females face while vibrating his wings frantically. This is his big act for attention.

Wildly impressed, the female agrees to mate and then leaves immediately afterwards to attend to the nest which is on the ground or close with a side tunnel entrance, comprised of grasses and stems of flowers and weeds, lined with soft down.

In this nest she lays 2 to 3 speckled brown eggs.

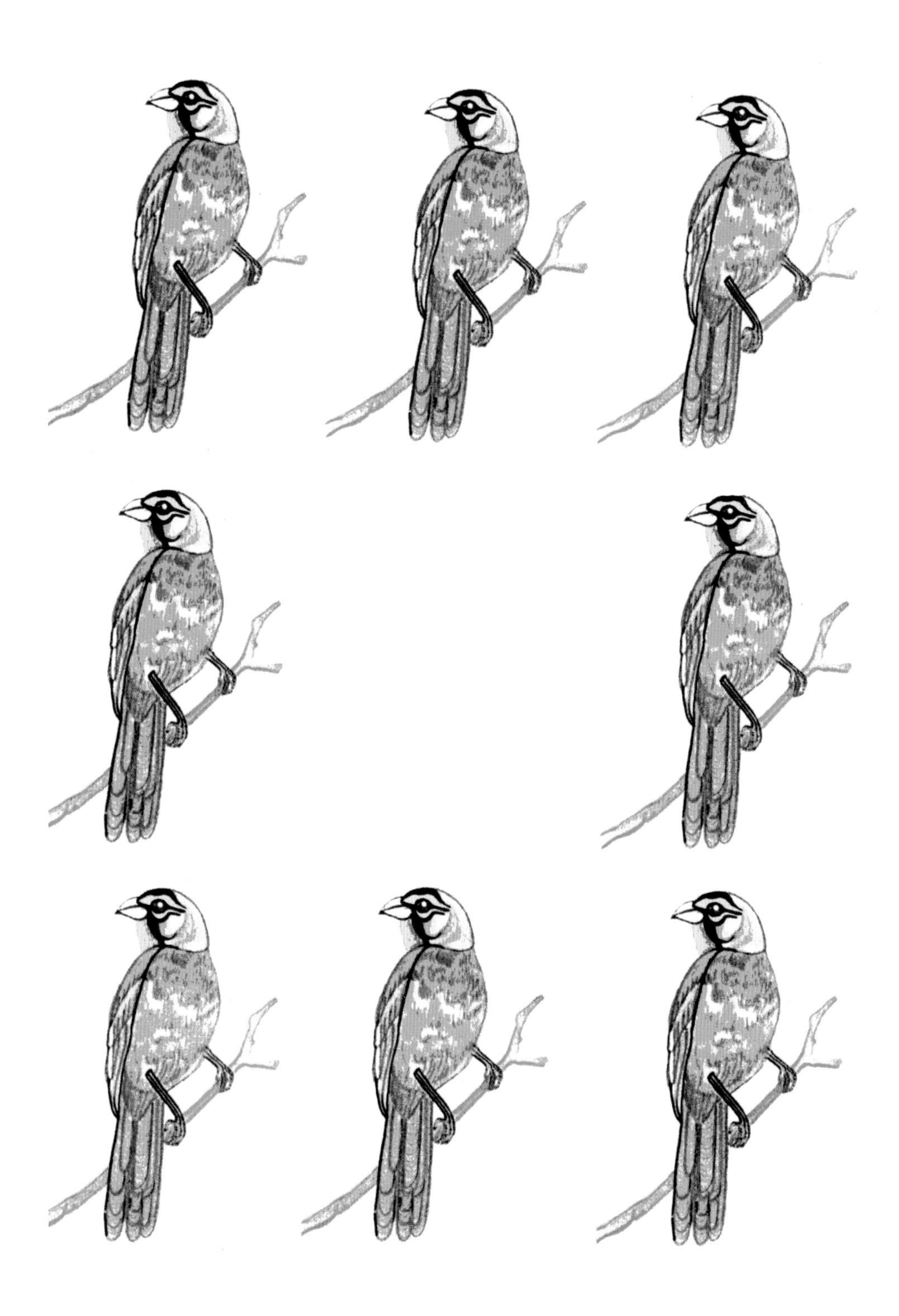

Lucy with Rebecca whom she bought 25 yrs. ago in St.Maarten.

Lucy Baker was born in Berkeley, California and hoped to never leave, but her parents divorce meant a move to Washington,D.C. for her stepfather's position with the U.S. government.

Lucy is well traveled and has lived in London & Europe. In 1938 & 1939 she attended school in Wurzburg, Germany. Her mother was a war-bride, marrying Walter Henry Baker who is proud of his Cherokee connection and is a direct descendant of Founding Father William Grayson, about whom Lucy has written.

Lucy has been involved in the Arts her entire life. She sang opera, was a soloist with the Washington Concert Ballet and has-painted and been a designer since she was a small girl.

She has been writing for many years now and has six children and eleven grandchildren scattered about the United States.

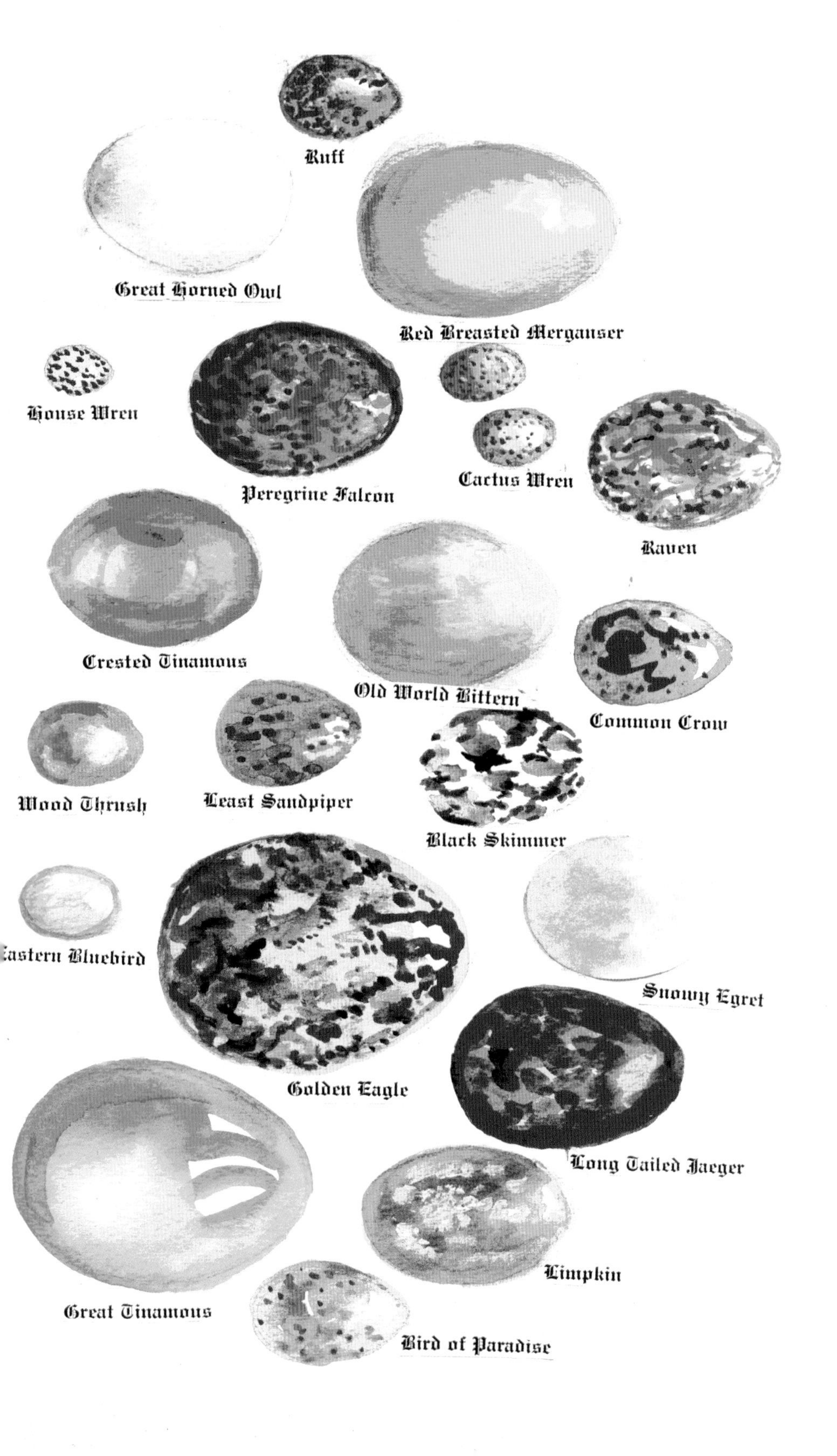
Ruff
Great Horned Owl
Red Breasted Merganser
House Wren
Peregrine Falcon
Cactus Wren
Raven
Crested Tinamous
Old World Bittern
Common Crow
Wood Thrush
Least Sandpiper
Black Skimmer
astern Bluebird
Snowy Egret
Golden Eagle
Long Tailed Jaeger
Limpkin
Great Tinamous
Bird of Paradise

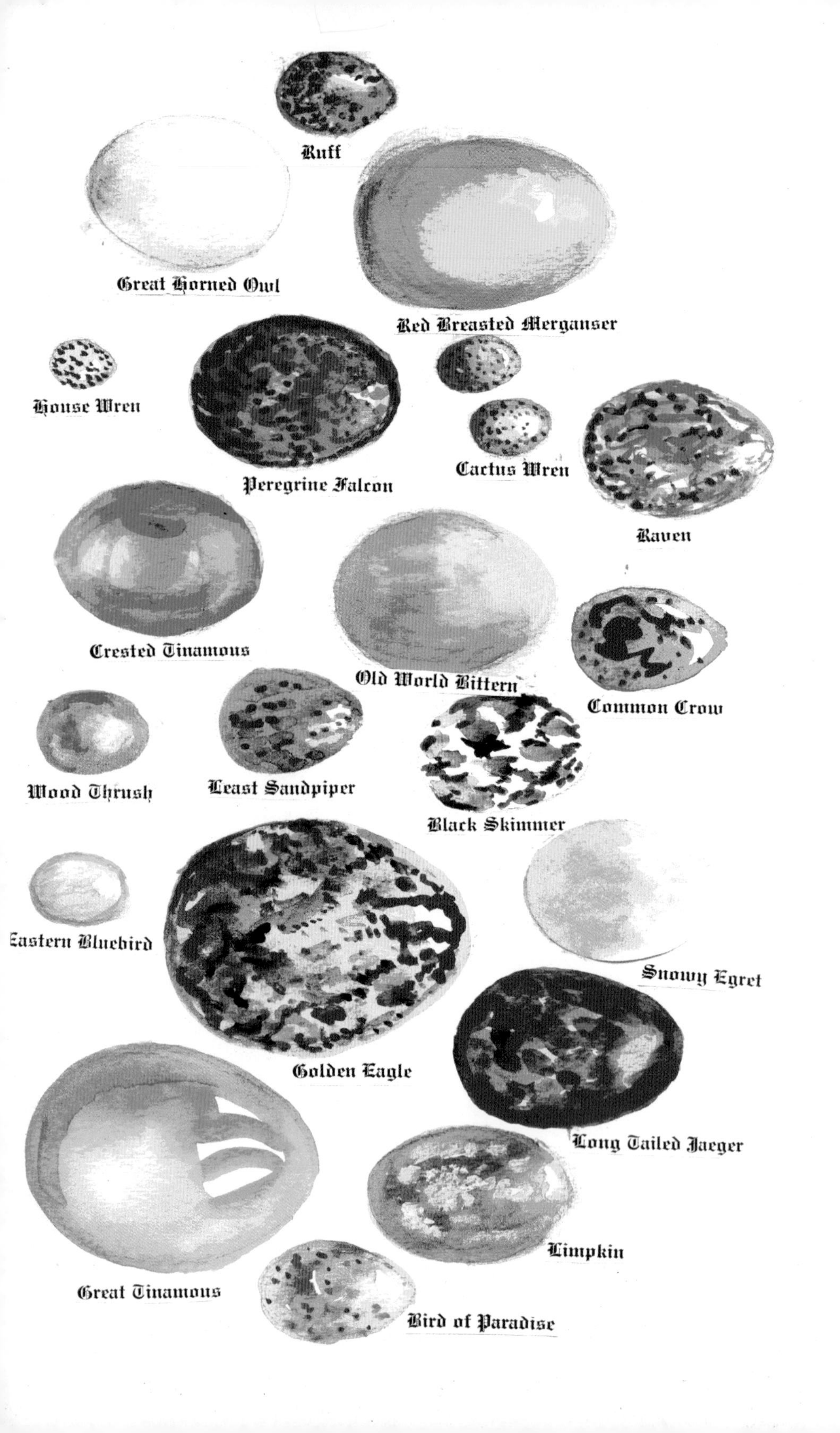
Ruff
Great Horned Owl
Red Breasted Merganser
House Wren
Peregrine Falcon
Cactus Wren
Raven
Crested Tinamous
Old World Bittern
Common Crow
Wood Thrush
Least Sandpiper
Black Skimmer
Eastern Bluebird
Snowy Egret
Golden Eagle
Long Tailed Jaeger
Limpkin
Great Tinamous
Bird of Paradise